United States
Department of the Interior
Bureau of Land Management

BLM Natural Resource Damage Assessment
and Restoration Handbook

THIS PAGE INTENTIONALLY LEFT BLANK

1.   OVERVIEW

1.1   INTRODUCTION

This Handbook provides guidance and policy that the U.S. Department of the Interior (DOI) Bureau of Land Management (BLM) personnel should follow when undertaking Natural Resource Damage Assessment and Restoration (NRDAR) activities. The BLM is responsible for sustaining the health, diversity, and productivity of the BLM-managed land under its jurisdiction for the use and enjoyment of present and future generations. The Federal Land Policy and Management Act (FLPMA) of 1976, Public Law 94-579, (43 U.S.C. 1701 et seq.) requires that the BLM provide the public the opportunity to use and appreciate significant cultural and natural resources while protecting and conserving them (FLPMA; 135 Departmental Manual 1, 1.3, A-D). Pursuant to these responsibilities, the resource management goals of the BLM are to maintain the health of the land and, to the best of its ability, to restore or replace resources that are harmed by pollution. The authorities and process of NRDAR are very useful tools for the BLM to use in accomplishing these resource stewardship responsibilities. The NRDAR authorities enable the BLM to seek compensation for restoration of injured resources (see Definitions and Terminology, Section 1.3) from the potentially responsible party (PRP) to fund restoration, but NRDAR injury assessment and restoration planning steps also can be a part of the BLM site activities that are funded by the BLM.

When the release (or the threat of a release) of hazardous substances or a discharge of oil harms the BLM-managed land or BLM-managed natural resources, and when response actions will not sufficiently restore the affected resources, the BLM and other Federal, State, and Tribal natural resource managers are authorized to seek damages from the PRP to restore the resources. The Comprehensive Environmental Response, Compensation, and Liability Act (CERCLA) of 1980, the Clean Water Act (CWA) of 1972, and the Oil Pollution Act (OPA) of 1990 provide a process for NRDAR activities that:

- Identify and quantify the adverse effect, or "injury," to natural resources caused by a release;
- Identify the actions needed to restore or replace the injured resources; and
- Seek damages from the PRP to pay for the restoration, and also the costs of assessing the restoration needs.

CERCLA and OPA response actions are intended to minimize risks to public health and welfare, and the environment.[1] NRDAR actions are intended to restore or replace natural resources. Response actions and NRDAR often can be integrated to save time, labor, and money, and to maximize efficiency in sustaining the health, diversity, and productivity of the BLM-managed land.

This Handbook provides the BLM policy for NRDAR, its statutory basis, the relationship between NRDAR and response actions, and steps for integrating the two processes. This Handbook also provides guidance to field staff and technicians on how to determine whether NRDAR is necessary, and if so, how to manage and conduct NRDAR.

The guidance provided herein cannot be relied on as legal advice, but should be used in conjunction with other guidance and relevant handbooks, applicable laws and regulations, and consultation from the Office of the Solicitor.

---

1. BLM procedures for CERCLA response actions are described in the CERCLA Response Actions Handbook No.1703-1.

1.2   PURPOSE OF NRDAR

The purpose of the NRDAR process is to enable Federal and State government agencies and Indian tribes who manage land and natural resources as trustees to assess resource injuries and restore those affected resources. The trustees can use NRDAR to address only injuries and service losses caused by releases of hazardous substances or discharges of oil. Trustees cannot use NRDAR to address harm caused by physical damage, unless the physical damage is incurred during the response to a discharge or release; NRDAR does not directly protect human health or compensate for private losses.

The NRDAR provisions of CERCLA, the CWA, and OPA are based on three key principles:

1.   Public natural resources are common property of all citizens. The Federal and State governments and tribes act as trustees of these resources on behalf of the public.

2.   The parties responsible for the hazardous substance release or oil spill are liable for the costs of restoring the injured resources and compensating the public for the public losses because of the release or spill until resource restoration is complete.

3.   The trustees may use any damages recovered from responsible parties through the NRDAR process only to restore, replace, or acquire the equivalent resources for the public trust.

Purpose of NRDAR: An Example

The purpose of NRDAR is to restore public natural resources injured or destroyed by releases of hazardous substances or oil spills, and to compensate the public for losses of the natural resource services that result from the releases or spills. This restoration can be the restoration, replacement or rehabilitation of injured resources and services, or the acquisition of the equivalent natural resources and services. The costs of the restoration are borne by the parties who are responsible for the release or spill.

For example, releases of acid mine drainage and toxic metals to the Sacramento River watershed from the Iron Mountain Mine Superfund Site in northern California caused risk to human health and the environment. In settlement, the responsible party agreed to pay for extensive site remediation. In addition, the responsible party paid $11 million for natural resource damages. The natural resource damages obtained in the settlement are being used to restore endangered salmon by removing dams to increase spawning habitat in the Sacramento River watershed, and to construct trails and increase recreation access on the BLM-managed land that had been closed to the public because of the contamination dangers at the Superfund site. The damages also are reimbursing the resource trustees for the cost of the assessment work that identified the restoration actions that would be necessary to address the natural resource (salmon) injuries and service losses (public recreation).

Iron Mountain Mine in Northern California

1.3   DEFINITIONS, TERMINOLOGY, AND ACRONYMS

1.3.1   Definitions and Terminology

This section provides a glossary of terms that are important to defining and understanding NRDAR.

Affected Bureau. A bureau that regards itself as being "affected," meaning that it has resource interests at a site and wishes to participate in site-specific NRDAR activities.

Authorized Official (AO). The manager from a Bureau, involved in a NRDAR case, which represents the trusteeship interests of the Secretary of the Interior to conduct natural resource damage assessment, restoration planning and implementation, in coordination with other agencies involved in the case.

Baseline Condition. The condition or conditions of a natural resource that would have existed at the assessment area had the discharge of oil or release of hazardous substance under investigation not occurred. The baseline condition is not necessarily the pristine or optimal condition and should take into account impacts on resources not related to the release.

Acid Mine Drainage on Spring Creek, Iron Mountain Mine, Redding, California

BLM Trusteeship. The BLM acts as a "trustee" on behalf of the Secretary of the Interior for natural resources managed or controlled by the BLM. These resources include: individual natural resources such as soils and sediments, plants, fisheries, birds, and wildlife; and habitats such as wetlands and riparian, aquatic, and upland habitats. The BLM asserts trusteeship for the services provided by these natural resources, such as recreational, cultural, scenic, and scientific uses. The BLM also asserts trusteeship for access to or availability of legally recognized consumptive uses of surface water and ground water and to the Federal mineral estate.

Case. Site-specific NRDAR activities are "cases" because they ultimately involve a legal element, either a court-approved settlement with, or litigation against, a PRP. CERCLA response activities are commonly said to occur at "sites" and OPA response activities occur as a result of "incidents."

Compensable Value. The value of actions undertaken to compensate public losses pending restoration. Related to "compensatory restoration" and "damages."

Compensatory Restoration. This refers to actions that compensate for public losses that accrue during the time between the discovery of the injury and its restoration to baseline condition. This time period may begin at the time the resource injury or service loss begins, depending on legal considerations. Compensatory restoration is often conducted in lieu of or in addition to primary restoration to baseline condition. Compensatory restoration might include restoration of the injured resources to greater than baseline condition, provision of additional services on-site, or restoration, rehabilitation, replacement, or acquisition of equivalent resources or services off-site ("restoration"). Related to "compensable value" and "damages," and distinguished from "baseline" or "primary" restoration, as defined by OPA.

Damages. A legal term for the amount of money sought in a claim made by trustee plaintiffs to PRP defendants; it includes the cost of assessing injuries as well as the cost of restoration implementation. Past damages accrue from the earliest point that injuries from releases can be determined, or authorization of the statute (e.g., December 1980 for CERCLA), up to the present. Future damages can include interim damages (from the present until restoration actions are completed and baseline condition is restored).

Discounting. An economic procedure that recognizes immediate benefits over delayed or future benefits. Discounting accounts for differences in the value of money today and either the past (greater value per dollar in the past) or the future (lesser value per dollar in the future). Discounting converts benefits or costs from different times such that they are comparable with each other.

Abandoned mine tailings, waste rock, debris, and acid mine drainage in the Arkansas River Watershed in Central Colorado

Emergency Restoration. An immediate action that must be taken to avoid an irreversible loss of natural resources, to prevent or reduce continuing danger to natural resources, or abate an emergency situation.

Ephemeral Data. Data or information about site conditions or resources that may be available only temporarily and would be lost if not collected immediately, because of dilution, movement, decomposition, leaching, or other factors.

Expedited NRDAR. Achieving restoration at a site through NRDAR without implementing the entire regulatory NRDAR process. For a particular case, restoration planning or restoration actions may be completed without fully implementing NRDAR assessment steps such as the injury determination, quantification, or damages determination phases described in the full NRDAR regulatory process. Expedited NRDAR may be possible, for example, through cooperative agreement with PRPs (see Section 4 of this Handbook), or when restoration needs are known without conducting a full assessment.

Habitat preservation to restore injured Marbled Murrelets: old growth forest, coastal Oregon

Exposure. Contact between a hazardous substance, by-product, or oil and a natural resource. Exposure does not constitute an injury, but exposure to a hazardous substance is necessary to cause an injury.

Habitat. The physical, chemical, and biological attributes that together provide basic needs for plant and animal species and communities of organisms. Habitat components include temperature, moisture, light, structural features (e.g., stream banks, tree canopy), food sources, and nesting, hiding, and thermal cover. The term can be used to define surroundings on almost any scale from very large regions to very small microhabitats.

Habitat Equivalency Analysis (HEA). An accounting model used to calculate the ecological service losses from past, ongoing, and future injuries (the debit side of the model) and the future service gains from proposed restoration needed to equal the debit (the credit side of the model). The HEA is used in cases of habitat injury when the service of the injured area is ecologically equivalent to the service that will be provided by the replacement habitat.

Hazardous Substances. Under CERCLA, "hazardous substances," as defined at 40 CFR §300.5, refer to some 800 toxic substances including metals, organics, solvents, and pesticides, as listed at 40 CFR §302.4, Table 302.4 List of Hazardous Substances and Reportable Quantities. The CWA lists additional hazardous substances at 40 CFR §116.5, Table 116.4.

Injury. Under OPA, injury is defined as an observable or measurable adverse change in a natural resource or impairment of a natural resource service. Injuries can occur directly or indirectly. Categories of injury include, but are not limited to, adverse changes in survival, growth, and reproduction; health, physiology, and biological conditions; behavior; community composition; ecological processes and functions; physical and chemical habitat quality or structure; and public services.

Under CERCLA, injury is defined similarly, as a measurable adverse effect on the physical, biological, or chemical quality of a natural resource. Specific injuries are defined in CERCLA NRDAR regulations at 43 CFR §11.62 for the following five categories of natural resources:

♦ Air;

♦ Biological resources;

♦ Ground water;

♦ Surface water resources including water, suspended sediments, and sediments comprising the beds, banks, and shoreline of a surface water body; and

♦ Geologic resources, including soils, subsurface materials, and other sediments.

Grand Mogul Mine in SW Colorado

Injury Scoping. Activities conducted during the removal site evaluation portion of the response process for a release of hazardous substances or oil spill, to determine the following:

Metals-Laden tailings on eroding bank of Pine Creek, Coeur d'Alene Basin, Idaho

- If natural resource injuries have resulted from the release or spill;
- If restoration is needed that can be integrated into the response actions; or
- If a subsequent natural resource damage assessment is necessary to sufficiently restore resources or services.

Interim Loss. The loss of natural resource services over a period of time, such as from the onset of resource injury, or the beginning of trustee authority to claim damages (promulgation of CERCLA in December 1980), until the return of the resource to its baseline condition, whether by restoration actions or natural recovery.

National Contingency Plan. The National Oil and Hazardous Substance Pollution Contingency Plan (NCP), promulgated by EPA pursuant to Section 105 of CERCLA and codified in 40 CFR Part 300.

Natural Resource. Surface water, sediments, soils, subsurface materials—including ground water and geologic materials, biota—including plants and animals, habitats on which biota depend, and air.

Pathway. The route or medium through which a hazardous substance travels from the point of release to the injured resource.

Potentially Responsible Party (PRP). A person or entity believed to have liability for response costs and/or natural resource damages, under the law, for a CERCLA release or an OPA oil spill.

Pollutant. Any element, compound, substance, or mixture, as defined by Section 101(33) of CERCLA that, after release into the environment and upon exposure to any organism, either directly or indirectly, does, or may be anticipated to, cause injury to such organisms or their offspring. See also *hazardous substance*.

Primary Restoration. Actions that restore, replace, rehabilitate, or acquire the equivalent of the injured natural resources. Sometimes called "baseline" restoration because actions bring injured resources back to baseline condition.

Removal Site Evaluation (RSE). The evaluation of a CERCLA site early in the response process for the purpose of planning and conducting removal actions. The RSE typically precedes the more comprehensive remedial process that may be necessary at a site.

Resource Equivalency Analysis (REA). An accounting model used to calculate the ecological service losses from past, ongoing, and future injuries (the debit side of the model) and the future service gains from proposed restoration needed to equal the debit (the credit side of the model). Specifically used for scaling losses of fish, birds, other biota, and other natural resources.

Restoration. Actions that accomplish the restoration, rehabilitation, replacement, and/or acquisition of equivalent resources and that are intended to return injured resources and services to baseline condition, and compensate the public for interim losses. Restoration can include actions that improve the quality of natural resources off-site and/or out-of-kind to address cumulative losses of resources or services over time as a result of the injury.

Services. Natural resources provide ecological and human services. Examples of ecological services include nutrient cycling, habitat, water storage and release, and erosion control. Examples of human use services include recreational use (e.g., fishing, hiking, bird watching), and extractive and consumptive use (e.g., mining, grazing), as well as non-active uses like the appreciation people feel knowing that habitat is protected for wildlife and for enjoyment by future generations of people.

Trustee Council. The formal group of representatives from agencies that are trustees, under CERCLA or OPA, for resources or services affected at a NRDAR site. Normally on the basis of a Memorandum of Understanding (MOU), the Council conducts NRDAR activities to obtain monetary damages to restore injured natural resources under their jurisdictions, and to plan, implement and oversee restoration.

1.3.2 Acronyms

ALC	aquatic life criteria
AO	authorized official
AP	Assessment Plan
AR	administrative record
ARAR	Applicable or Relevant and Appropriate Requirements
BIA	Bureau of Indian Affairs
BLM	Bureau of Land Management
CA	cost analysis
CAA	Clean Air Act
CCC	criterion continuous concentration
CERCLA	Comprehensive Environmental Response, Compensation, and Liability Act
CMC	criterion maximum concentration
CNTS	covenant not to sue
CWA	Federal Water Pollution Control Act (Clean Water Act)
CX	categorical exclusion
DARP	Damage Assessment and Restoration Plan
DOC	U.S. Department of Commerce
DOD	U.S. Department of Defense
DOE	U.S. Department of Energy
DOI	U.S. Department of the Interior
DOJ	U.S. Department of Justice
DPA	Deepwater Ports Act
DSAY	discounted service acre-year
DSRS	Division of Science and Resource Services
EA	environmental assessment
EE	engineering evaluation
EIS	environmental impact statement
EPA	U.S. Environmental Protection Agency
FIFRA	Federal Insecticide, Fungicide, and Rodenticide Act
FLPMA	Federal Land Policy and Management Act
FONSI	finding of no significant impact
FWS	U.S. Fish & Wildlife Service
HEA	habitat equivalency analysis
IAG	Interagency Agreement
LAT	Lead Administrative Trustee
MCL	maximum contaminant level
MCLG	MCL goal
MIS	Management Information Systems
MOA	Memorandum of Agreement
MOU	Memorandum of Understanding
MPRSA	Marine Protection, Research, and Sanctuaries Act

NCP	National Oil and Hazardous Substances Pollution Contingency Plan
NEPA	National Environmental Policy Act
NOAA	National Oceanic and Atmospheric Administration
NOC	National Operations Center
NOI	Notice of Intent
NPDES	National Pollutant Discharge Elimination System
NPFC	U.S Coast Guard National Pollution Fund Center
NPL	National Priorities List
NPS	National Park Service
NPSRA	National Park System Resources Protection Act
NRDAR	natural resource damage assessment and restoration
NRIS	natural resource injury scoping
OPA	Oil Pollution Act
PAS	Pre-Assessment Screen
PASD	Pre-Assessment Screen Determination
PEC	probable effect concentration
PED	Preliminary Estimate of Damages
PRFA	Pollution Removal Funding Agreement
PRP	potentially responsible party
QAPP	Quality Assurance Project Plan
RCDP	restoration and compensation determination plan
RCRA	Resource Conservation and Recovery Act
REA	resource equivalency analysis
REO	Regional Environmental Officer
RMP	Resource Management Plan
RSE	Removal Site Evaluation
SARA	Superfund Amendments and Reauthorization Act
SDWA	Safe Drinking Water Act
SDWRs	secondary drinking water regulations
SI	site inspection
SIPC	special interest project code
SRSD	Science and Resource Services Division
SWDA	Solid Waste Disposal Act
TAPAA	Trans-Alaska Pipeline Authorization Act
TEC	threshold effect concentration
USACE	U.S. Army Corps of Engineers
USBR	U.S. Bureau of Reclamation
USDA	U.S. Department of Agriculture
USGS	U.S. Geological Survey
WO	Washington Office

1.4   THE BLM ACTING AS A NATURAL RESOURCE TRUSTEE

Section 107(f)(1) of CERCLA and Section 1006(c) of OPA authorize the United States to act on behalf of the public as a natural resource trustee; the NCP (40 CFR §300.600) designates the Secretary of the Interior to act as a natural resource trustee.

What are "natural resources"?

Under the NRDAR regulations, natural resources are defined broadly to include land, fish, wildlife, biota, air, water, ground water, drinking water supplies and other resources managed or controlled by an agency. Under this definition, resources managed or controlled by the BLM include soils, sediments, geologic structures, plants, fisheries, birds and wildlife components of wetland, riparian, aquatic, and upland environments and the natural, ecological habitats that they form. Natural resources also include leasable and other minerals resources.

The BLM acts on behalf of the Secretary and asserts trusteeship for natural resources under its jurisdiction, management, or control. The natural resource categories are air, surface water, ground water, geologic resources (i.e., soils), and biological resources. The BLM jurisdiction includes public losses associated with the use of surface water and ground water and the BLM-administered fluid and solid minerals resources. Therefore, releases of oil or hazardous substances that adversely affect the public's ability to access leasable minerals, or to prospect or claim for locatable minerals or mineral materials (e.g., sand, gravel, and stone) may trigger NRDAR to compensate for the loss of access to public resources.

The BLM-managed natural resources also provide important human and ecological services such as fishing, hunting, recreation, grazing, and minerals production, and non-uses such as public appreciation of the existence of a wilderness area. Natural resources also provide ecological services such as wildlife habitat, flood and erosion control, and water supply. Impacts from hazardous substances or oil may result in the reduction of these types of services. Parties

Restoration Costs

Restoration costs include the costs for actions to restore, replace, rehabilitate, or acquire the equivalent of injured resources and compensate for lost resource services.

responsible for releases of hazardous substances or oil are liable for the cost (or value) of restoration, compensation for public losses pending restoration, and reasonable assessment costs.

1.5   WHEN NRDAR MAY BE APPROPRIATE

If BLM-managed natural resources have or may have been injured as a result of contamination by hazardous substance releases or oil spill incidents, the BLM may determine to undertake damage assessment activities. For CERCLA sites or OPA incidents where the BLM is not the lead response agency, the BLM may be invited to consider initiating NRDAR activities based on preliminary evaluation of suspected impacts to BLM resources with or without natural resource injury scoping.[2]

For CERCLA sites or OPA incidents where the BLM is the lead response agency, the BLM conducts response actions to minimize risk to human health and the environment. In addition to response actions at a site, the BLM may also conduct natural resource injury scoping when it suspects natural resource injuries including service losses. The BLM should consider conducting NRDAR activities after the injury scoping under any of the following circumstances:

◆   **Response Action without Sufficient Restoration**. Restoration needs are known, but natural resources are not restored or replaced by response actions, or significant injury or loss of services occurs because of delays in response actions.

---

2. Injury scoping is described in the BLM CERCLA Response Actions Handbook, Chapter 4.

◆ **Injury without Response Actions**. Injury scoping identifies resource injury and restoration is deemed necessary to return resources to baseline, even if response actions are deemed unnecessary.

◆ **New Injury from Response Actions**. Injury scoping identifies that response actions will result in additional new resource injury or service loss; thus, assessment activities are needed to identify the extent of new injury, and on-site restoration actions cannot be accomplished until after the completion of the response action.

◆ **Restoration Needs Unknown during Response**. Injury scoping identifies resource injury for which it is appropriate to conduct restoration, but the restoration actions are not yet identified or cannot be incorporated into the on-site response actions; thus, later, separate restoration actions may be necessary.

◆ **Service Losses Unaddressed by Response**. Injury scoping determines that there will be significant service losses that cannot be characterized during injury scoping to identify the needed compensation, or addressed by the removal action. In such cases, NRDAR activities will be needed at a later time to identify the full extent of service losses and compensatory restoration needs, or to conduct the compensatory restoration.

Under any of the above circumstances, the BLM may elect to conduct NRDAR activities after injury scoping if its resource interests and those of other DOI bureaus or agencies are such that conducting cooperative NRDAR activities would result in the most beneficial restoration.

1.6 NRDAR AUTHORITIES

1.6.1 Statutes and Regulations

The following are the primary statutes and regulations authorizing NRDAR:

◆ CERCLA, as amended (42 U.S.C. 9601, et seq.);

◆ CWA, as amended (33 U.S.C. 1251, et seq.);

◆ OPA (33 U.S.C. 2701, et seq.) ; and

◆ NCP (40 CFR Part 300).

NRDAR procedures are provided for in the NCP at 40 CFR Part 300, the NRDAR regulations at 43 CFR Part 11, and OPA NRDAR regulations at 15 CFR Part 990. The OPA regulations are supplemented by National Oceanic and Atmospheric Administration (NOAA) guidance documents (NOAA-Damage Assessment and Restoration Plan (DARP), 1996).

43 CFR Part 11 provides procedures for determining injuries to natural resources. These regulations apply when the environment is harmed by a release of hazardous substances. Hazardous substances are defined in Section 101(14) of CERCLA and listed in Table 302.4, List of Hazardous Substances and Reportable Quantities, 40 CFR §302.4.

The CERCLA legislation incorporates a broad exclusion that prevents defining petroleum and natural gas products, both unrefined and refined, as hazardous substances under CERCLA. In addition, the Resource Conservation and Recovery Act (RCRA) exempts certain wastes intrinsic to crude oil and natural gas exploration and production processes from regulation as RCRA subtitle "C" hazardous waste (see: http://www.epa.gov/epaoswer/other/oil/oil-gas.pdf). The exemption applies only to the Federal requirements of RCRA Subtitle C. A waste that is exempt from RCRA Subtitle C regulation might be subject to more stringent or broader State hazardous and non-hazardous waste regulations and other State and Federal program regulations. For example, oil and gas exploration and production wastes are subject to regulation under the Clean Air Act (CAA), CWA, Safe Drinking Water Act (SDWA), and OPA.

OPA regulations apply when oil or petroleum products are discharged to waters of the United States causing harm to natural resources. Recent EPA and U.S. Army Corps of Engineers (USACE) guidance interpreting what is meant by the term "Waters of the U.S." can be found using the current link: http://www.epa.gov/owow/wetlands/pdf/RapanosGuidance6507.pdf.

1.6.2   DOI and BLM NRDAR Authorities, Policies, and References

It is DOI policy (DM 521) that bureaus "conduct NRDAR activities in accordance with the regulations under CERCLA (43 CFR Part 11) and OPA (15 CFR Part 990) to the greatest extent practicable, and develop and maintain an Administrative Record (AR) of actions taken during the assessment, restoration planning, and restoration process."

Delegation of Authority

The NCP designates to Federal and State agencies and federally recognized Indian tribes the authority to act as trustees for public resources. The Secretary of the Interior has delegated this authority within the Department to the Directors of the resource-managing bureaus to act on behalf of the DOI to carry out trusteeship for resources in their jurisdictions.

The Director of the BLM has delegated primary NRDAR authorities to the State Directors. The State Director acts as the authorized official (AO) if the BLM requests to be the DOI lead on a case. If a BLM State Office wishes to be delegated as the DOI AO for a specific case affecting BLM resources, the office should contact the Science and Resource Services Division at the National Operations Center or the Washington Office (WO) to arrange the AO request.

Within the BLM, the Delegation of Authority Manual 1203 identifies who in the BLM can make decisions and when that authority may be delegated to another entity within the BLM.

DOI policy documents relevant to NRDAR include the Departmental Manual, Part 207, Chapter 6, "Natural Resource Damage Assessment and Restoration" (207 DM 6) and Departmental Manual, Part 521, Chapter 1, "Authorities and Policy;" Chapter 2, "Responsibilities;" and Chapter 3, "Signatory Authority." Links to these Manuals and a description of the DOI NRDAR program and policies can be found at: http://restoration.doi.gov/policies.html.

The following BLM NRDAR policies are consistent with DOI NRDAR policies and provide specific guidance to the BLM staff working at sites contaminated by CERCLA hazardous substances or OPA oil spills. In accordance with this guidance, the BLM shall:

1. Expedite restoration of natural resources managed by the BLM by integrating actions to restore injured natural resources and their services into CERCLA and OPA response actions, wherever possible.

2. Consider both the injuries to natural resources managed by the BLM and losses of services provided by those natural resources when determining whether to conduct NRDAR activities or seek damages.

3. Determine natural resource damages based on the cost or value of the restoration actions necessary to restore or replace the injured resource and provide compensatory resource services pending restoration, rather than on the intrinsic value of the injured resources, wherever possible.

4. Notify the appropriate DOI contact—normally the Regional Environmental Officer (REO), other potentially affected trustee agencies, and appropriate response agencies—promptly when the BLM verifies a potential need for undertaking NRDAR activities related to BLM-managed natural resources or services.

5. Seek to involve representatives of all BLM programs whose resource jurisdictions are affected at sites warranting BLM NRDAR activities.

6. Coordinate BLM NRDAR activities as closely as possible with all other trustees, including other DOI bureaus, Federal agencies, States, and tribes, acting as natural resource trustees or conducting response actions.

7. Conduct BLM NRDAR activities in accordance with CERCLA NRDAR regulations at 43 CFR Part 11, and OPA NRDAR regulations at 15 CFR Part 990. Following published NRDAR guidance, regulations, and policy should help the BLM staff pursue a formal NRDAR and settlement negotiations or litigation, if necessary.[3]

8. Comply with existing safety and site entry policies of the BLM in the conduct of NRDAR activities at CERCLA and OPA sites.

9. Track the costs of site-specific NRDAR activities through the use of dedicated NRDAR codes and cost tracking forms and seek cost avoidance or cost recovery.

1.7   THE BLM AND OTHER TRUSTEE AGENCIES

1.7.1 DOI Bureaus

DOI bureaus that may be co-trustees with the BLM are the U.S. Fish & Wildlife Service (FWS), the Bureau of Indian Affairs (BIA), the U.S. Bureau of Reclamation (USBR), and the National Park Service (NPS). The U.S. Geological Survey (USGS) provides technical support to the five DOI bureaus. The FWS trusteeship pertains to all lands, focusing on anadromous fish, migratory birds, and threatened or endangered species, and to national refuges. The BIA trusteeship relates to the reserved lands, resources and cultural practices of American Indian tribes. The USBR and NPS trusteeships relate to their established facilities, parks, and monuments.

1.7.2 Other Federal, State, and Tribal Trustees

The NCP (40 CFR §300.600) designates the Secretaries of the U.S. Department of Agriculture (USDA), U.S. Department of Commerce (DOC), U.S. Department of Defense (DOD), and U.S. Department of Energy (DOE), as well as the DOI, to act as Federal trustees for natural resources. In addition to the United States, CERCLA and OPA authorize the States to act as trustees for lands in their respective State. Indian tribes are authorized to act as trustees for the natural resources, including their supporting ecosystems, belonging to, managed by, controlled by, or appertaining to such Indian tribe, or held in trust for the benefit of such Indian tribe, or belonging to a member of such Indian tribe, if such resources are subject to a trust restriction on alienation (CERCLA 107(f) (1); OPA 1006(c) and section 311(f) (5) of the CWA).

Resources under the trusteeship of USDA include federally managed rangelands, fisheries, farmlands, lands enrolled in the Wetlands Reserve Program, and national forest lands. Offices overseeing these resources include the U.S. Forest Service, the U.S. Natural Resources Conservation Service, and the Conservation Reserve Program.

Resources under the trusteeship of DOC include coastal environments, estuarine research reserves, marine sanctuaries, endangered marine species, marine mammals, and rivers that historically supported or presently support anadromous fish. Trustee responsibility in DOC is delegated to NOAA. Offices or groups within NOAA that have trustee responsibilities include the National Marine Fisheries Service, the Office of Ocean and Coastal Resource Management, the Office of Oceanography and Marine Services, and the Office of General Counsel.

The DOD has trusteeship over the natural resources on lands owned by the DOD, including the Army, Navy, Air Force, and Defense Logistics Agency. The Secretary of DOE has trusteeship over natural resources on the grounds of national research and development laboratories, facilities, and offices.

A State asserts trusteeship for natural resources and supporting ecosystems that belong to, are managed by, or

---

3. In cases where there is a MOU with the PRP that describes conditions of a cooperative arrangement to assess restoration needs and implement restoration, the BLM might consider processes other than those in the CERCLA or OPA NRDAR regulations. See Section 4 of this Handbook for further discussion of cooperative assessments.

appertain to the State (40 CFR §300.605). The governor of each State designates one or more State trustees and can delegate responsibility to any entity or entities. The designated official is often the head of an agency responsible for environmental health and protection, fish and wildlife management, or legal matters. Examples of State trust resources include State lands; State-owned minerals; State parks and monuments; biota (including State rare, threatened, and endangered species); State wildlife refuges and fish hatcheries; ground water; and surface water.

Tribal chair persons or heads of the governing bodies or their designees act as trustees for natural resources belonging to, managed by, controlled by, appertaining to, or held in trust for, an Indian tribe or a member of an Indian tribe (40 CFR §300.610). The Secretary of the Interior may act as trustee on behalf of a tribe at the tribe's request. Examples of resources under tribal trusteeship include tribal-owned minerals, ground water, and surface water resources on tribal lands, and any other natural resources found on tribal land.

1.7.3 Coordination with other Trustees and Response Agencies

If the discharge or release of oil or hazardous substances affects BLM resources and resources of other agencies, the BLM coordinates with those co-trustees in conducting NRDAR activities. As soon as it is apparent that NRDAR activities should be considered, the BLM should inquire regarding the designation of the Department of the Interior Authorized Official (see Section 2.1.2-2.1.4). Co-trustees can efficiently share the technical and administrative burden of injury assessment and restoration planning and thus reduce the effort by any single trustee agency. Pre-NRDAR planning can help identify co-trusteeship, contact persons, and agency teaming arrangements.

A trustee MOU should be established to foster coordination and cooperation between co-trustees participating on a NRDAR case. A trustee MOU is an essential component of a cost-effective damage assessment. The goals of such coordination are to avoid duplication, reduce costs, and achieve dual objectives where possible.

The MOU provides a structure for the trustee council and can identify the lead administrative trustee among the ranking managers of the involved agencies. The Lead Administrative Trustee (LAT) acts as the Coordinator[4] and contact regarding all aspects of the assessment. The LAT is not necessarily the DOI authorized official (AO). In some cases, an MOU can include the U.S. Environmental Protection Agency (EPA) or other response agencies that are closely involved in response or resource management at the site. The MOU might structure technical working groups, schedules, or other administrative details, and it might include confidentiality agreements to protect information developed individually or cooperatively by the participating trustees. An MOU also can define procedures for resolving conflicts between the parties to the MOU. Individual PRPs also might be co-signers to a trustee MOU as a basis for cooperation.

1.8 RELATIONSHIP BETWEEN NRDAR AND RESPONSE ACTIONS

The BLM policy is to integrate NRDAR actions to restore injured resources and replace lost services with CERCLA and OPA response actions, whenever it is possible and prudent. Close coordination of NRDAR and response actions, from site discovery through the removal or remedial action, can allow for timely data collection, maximize information gathering efficiency, save time and money, permit prompt notification of other trustee agencies and the PRP, and result in earlier completion of restoration. If process integration is not possible, the BLM should seek close coordination to maximize mutual benefits and enhance the effectiveness of NRDAR.

Much of the information collected during site verification and the response process may be useful for injury scoping and for the NRDAR Pre-Assessment. For example, during site verification, the BLM evaluates whether or not an oil spill or hazardous substance release has occurred, and whether it has or could significantly affect public lands or

---

4 In this Handbook, the BLM Coordinator is the staff person who conducts or oversees NRDAR activities.

resources managed by the BLM. The BLM identifies, if possible, the date, time, source, quantity and identity/content of the spill or release; the media affected by it; potential injuries to natural resources; and information about the PRP.

During the CERCLA Removal Site Evaluation (RSE) process, restoration needs identified during natural resource injury scoping can be considered and possibly incorporated in the removal actions. If a removal action can remove threats to public health and welfare or the environment, and also return resources rapidly to baseline condition, further NRDAR activities might not be necessary. This is the most efficient approach to maintaining the health of the land following a release of hazardous substances. If removal actions subsequently are found to be insufficient, NRDAR restoration could include additional removal actions. Applicable or Relevant and Appropriate Requirements (ARARs) that protect natural resources or services also may help to achieve restoration goals by influencing the cleanup actions.

If the BLM elects to implement the remedial response process because of complex contamination or site conditions, the NRDAR process may also be warranted. The remedial process may afford the BLM additional time to complete NRDAR activities, because this response status may extend the statute of limitations on trustees filing NRDAR claims against PRPs (see Section 3.4.6).

The OPA response following an oil spill often may proceed rapidly, at first under emergency conditions. NRDAR activities should also commence quickly and in conjunction and communication with the response. They should include organizing which resources are of concern to the BLM and other trustees, and determine what ephemeral data collection is immediately necessary. It is important to work with the response On-Scene Coordinator to minimize the time and cost of field activities, maximize data collection efficiency, and coordinate the interactions among cleanup activities, resource protection, and restoration actions.

Coordinating information collection and data sharing between the NRDAR and response processes is essential for maximizing site or incident cleanup and restoration goals coordination. The BLM should be attentive to the response investigations, ecological risk assessments, feasibility studies, response action schedules, and anticipated response action outcomes. There is likely to be information from them that the BLM can use for the injury assessment, the estimation of duration of service losses, and the quantification of damages that may remain after site response.

1.9 INTRODUCTION TO THE STEPS OF NATURAL RESOURCE RESTORATION

Natural resource restoration includes the following main steps:

◆ Pre-NRDAR Preparation – Coordination and Pre-incident Planning
◆ Natural Resource Injury Scoping (injured resource evaluation)
◆ Pre-Assessment Screen (determination to proceed)
◆ Natural Resource Damage Assessment, which includes:
   ▸ Assessment Plan;
   ▸ Injury Determination;
   ▸ Injury Quantification; and
   ▸ Damages Determination.
◆ Post-Assessment (Restoration Implementation and Monitoring)

Figure 1.1 shows the CERCLA and OPA NRDAR processes. Note that the CERCLA and OPA processes have different terminology for the various steps, but they have similar functional outcomes. There are differences for similar processes but the goal of both is resource restoration. The NRDAR process is described in further detail in Section 3.

Figure 1.1: Flowchart showing the processes of NRDAR activities under CERCLA and OPA

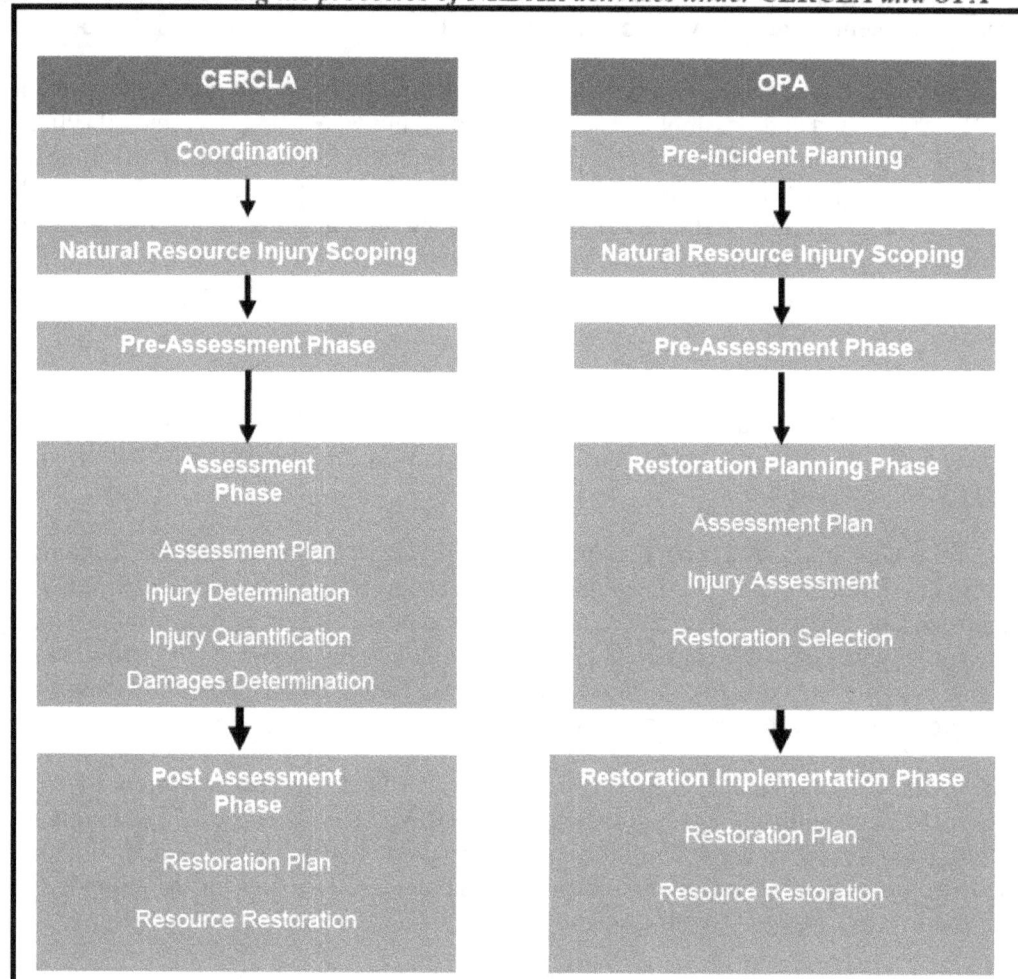

1.9.1   Pre-NRDAR Preparation

Pre-NRDAR preparation under both CERCLA and OPA involves pre-release or pre-incident coordination and planning. The goal is to be prepared, as much as possible, to react to releases and incidents in order to effectively address site conditions to minimize both harm to the environment and the costs of managing the event. Pre-NRDAR preparation should make use of existing, up-to-date contingency plans maintained by State and Field Offices, supplemented by other trustee contact information, process steps to initiate NRDAR activities, and other relevant information (see Section 3.2).

1.9.2   Injury Scoping

During the injury-scoping phase, the BLM should closely coordinate injury scoping with response activities. During this phase, the Coordinator evaluates whether resource injuries have occurred at the site, and if so, whether response actions will sufficiently restore the injured resources.[5] If there are restoration needs that cannot be incorporated into the removal actions and further NRDAR activities are needed, then the Pre-Assessment phase begins.

---

5. The CERCLA Response Actions Handbook, Chapter 4, discusses the injury scoping process. See also Section 3.3 of this Handbook.

1.9.3 Pre-Assessment Screening

During the Pre-Assessment Screen (PAS) phase, the BLM Coordinator uses existing information to verify whether site conditions warrant NRDAR activities. In addition, the Coordinator evaluates whether sufficient data exist, or could be attained at reasonable cost, to determine the extent of the injury and actions needed to restore the resources and compensate for interim loss of services. In some situations, limited field sampling might be necessary during the PAS phase to preserve data and information that would be lost if it were not collected at that time. Such ephemeral data collection is typically limited to samples necessary to document the release and its acute effects. During the PAS phase, the BLM also should verify that at least one viable PRP for the site is approachable to pay NRDAR costs.

During the PAS, and at any time early in the NRDAR process, emergency actions may be necessary to restore resources or services that are of critical human use or ecological importance.

1.9.4 Assessment Planning and Implementation

If additional data are needed to determine the extent of injury caused by a release of hazardous substances or oil spill, or if analyses are needed to calculate the cost of restoration or the value of the service loss, then the trustees should plan and implement an assessment of injury and damages. The major assessment steps are the assessment plan (including a preliminary estimate of damages), injury determination, injury quantification, and damage determination, including preliminary restoration planning. Assessment planning ensures that data are collected in a planned and systematic manner, and that the methods can be conducted at reasonable cost.

During the CERCLA assessment phase, or the OPA restoration planning phase, the spatial and temporal extents and the degree of harm to natural resources should be quantified as part of injury determination and quantification. The amount and type of restoration actions needed to restore resources and to compensate for intervening losses are calculated as part of damage determination. In addition, the assessment includes the calculation of monetary damages for use in settlement proceedings or litigation against the PRP to seek payment for the damages.

1.9.5 Post-Assessment

A Report of Assessment is prepared during the post assessment phase to report the outcome of the assessment and to identify the needed restoration actions and estimated costs. This phase also includes the BLM legal representative sending the PRP a written demand for natural resource damages, (i.e., the costs of conducting the restoration and compensation actions, and the assessment costs the trustees have incurred). To obtain payment for the damages, the BLM may be able to negotiate a settlement with the PRP or litigate against them. The BLM then receives payment for the damages through settlement consent decree or a court ruling.

The post assessment phase includes the preparation of a restoration plan with public comment, followed by restoration design and engineering plans, restoration implementation, and long-term monitoring, maintenance, and documentation of the recovery of resources and services targeted by the restoration actions.

For Federal trustees, restoration planning under either CERCLA or OPA must proceed in accordance with the National Environmental Policy Act (NEPA), because a Federal action is being planned using Federal funds, (i.e., the receipts from the damages claim). The CERCLA and OPA NRDAR regulations also contain public involvement activities that are necessary at earlier process phases.

1.10 ALTERNATIVES TO THE FULL NRDAR PROCESS

The BLM may have an opportunity to achieve restoration at the site without implementing the entire regulatory NRDAR process. After the BLM has decided to conduct NRDAR activities, it may be prudent to conduct a modified assessment process to identify the natural resource restoration needs or resolve the damages claim cooperatively with the PRP. This could be termed an expedited NRDAR. Site conditions, data availability, and/or elements of potential PRP agreement, may indicate that such an approach could be the most effective to attain resource restoration. This type of expedited process may lead to settlement negotiations and the development of a settlement agreement or a consent decree that provides resolution of NRDAR claims. As with all legal matters, settlement negotiations should be fully coordinated with the Office of the Solicitor.

The BLM supports and encourages Coordinators to seek such cooperative arrangements (see Section 4). Examples of modifications to the NRDAR process would be agreeing on injuries, damages, or restoration needs without the full assessment. When an expedited NRDAR is not prudent, it is BLM policy to follow CERCLA and OPA regulations in conducting NRDAR activities.

2.   MANAGING NRDAR

2.1   NRDAR MANAGEMENT RESPONSIBILITIES

This section discusses the roles and responsibilities of the BLM Assistant Director (WO-200), State Directors and Field Office Managers in carrying out BLM NRDAR activities. It briefly describes the role of the DOI AO, the process of designation of the AO, and the involvement of the State Director related to the AO role. Specifically, this section identifies the various process steps and managerial decision points that involve BLM management. See BLM Manual 1703 for more information. Lastly, this section addresses the duties of the Coordinator in conducting NRDAR activities.

2.1.1   Assistant Director: Washington Office (WO)

The Assistant Director 200 serves as the BLM management representative to the Executive Board of the DOI Restoration Program. The Executive Board members direct the NRDAR activities within their respective bureaus and provide consensus management decisions regarding Restoration Program matters. The Restoration Program provides leadership and administrative support to the bureaus as they carry out NRDAR activities for cases around the country. In January or February of each year, the Board members approve annual DOI funding allocations for the bureaus' NRDAR cases, as well as program administration funding that supports the Restoration Program Office and the Work Group. The Work Group consists of bureau staff counterparts who serve part time in support of the Restoration Program Manager. The Executive Board also is called to periodic meetings to discuss and approve Restoration Program policy and related matters.

2.1.2   State Director

The State Directors have primary authority for specific BLM NRDAR cases, as delegated by the BLM Director in Instruction Memorandum 2001-061. The BLM Delegation of Authority Manual 1203 identifies which management level in the BLM can make NRDAR decisions. Most decisions reside with the State Director and may not be delegated to a lower level within the BLM. Case-specific activities involve the State Director annually and at specific points in the assessment process, such as the initiation of an assessment or the documentation of assessment plans and results. Specific points of involvement are listed in Table 2.1.

The State Director should note the need for <u>annual</u> involvement for NRDAR cases being conducted within the State, typically in late summer, to approve or concur with case-specific funding proposals that the involved DOI bureaus jointly submit to the DOI. The BLM may receive its funding for participating on a case through this joint proposal.

When the BLM becomes aware of a hazardous substance release or oil spill potentially affecting BLM-managed land or resources, the State Director should make the final decision as to whether BLM should conduct NRDAR activities, upon recommendation of the Field Office Manager. This BLM decision should be made on the basis of the BLM resources affected and in coordination with other bureaus and agencies that may have resource interests at the site.

Table 2.1 depicts the important phases and tasks of a fully implemented NRDAR process, as set out by the DOI NRDAR regulations, and the BLM management involvement in each phase. The table very briefly describes the outcomes of the tasks and the management decisions that flow from the tasks. The table follows the NRDAR process from before Pre-Assessment Screen (PAS) activities through post assessment activities. Several process steps involve the preparation of documents. The table shows whether the public or the PRPs should receive documents, denoted by an X, and be invited to review and comment on the documents, denoted by Y. When the BLM determines to undertake the process, the Coordinator should ensure that these process steps are carried out on behalf of BLM interests, according to the BLM case strategy. The Coordinator should garner the assistance of technical staff, economists, budgetary assistance, and attorney support from the DOI Solicitor's Office.

The table shows the respective NRDAR steps that could take place and require BLM decisions with respect to BLM trustee interests for a case. In most cases the BLM is likely to be a member of a trustee council with other agencies, and the BLM Coordinator may or may not be the case manager (see Section 2.4.2). In any case, the State Director, or Field Office Manager for injury scoping, has important decisions to make on behalf of BLM interests in the case. The Coordinator should ensure that the manager is apprised of case developments and prepared to make decisions regarding the respective tasks or case steps, or provide concurrences to the lead agency manager, as the case proceeds through the NRDAR process.

Table 2.1 NRDAR Phase, Task and Staff Conducting the Task, Purpose and Outcome of Task, Decision and Decision-Maker, and Involvement of the Public/PRP

NRDAR Phase	Task / Staff	Purpose	Outcome / Document	Decision / Manager	To PRP	To Public
Pre-PAS (done within response process)	Natural Resource Injury Scoping (NRIS) **Coordinator**	Early identification of restoration goals/actions to be included in removal action	**Injury Scoping Report**	**Field Manager** Whether restoration is completed, or go to PAS	Optional	Optional
Pre-PAS	Trustee MOU	Membership, organization, purpose of trustee council, confidentiality agreement	**Agreement on Trustee Cooperation, Council Leadership, member roles, data sharing**	**State Director** Approval of BLM involvement on trustee council		
Pre-Assessment Screen	PAS **Coordinator w/ Solicitor**	Evaluate if BLM should conduct NRDAR activities	**PAS Determination Report**	**State Director** BLM NRDAR activities warranted?	X	Optional
Pre-Assessment Screen	Notice of Intent to Conduct an Assessment **Solicitor w/ Coordinator**	Communication to PRPs of PAS decision and invite to cooperate	Letter	**State Director** BLM announcement to PRP, seeking cooperation	X	
Assessment	Preliminary Estimate of Damages (PED) **Coordinator w/ Economist and Solicitor**	Estimate potential damages, data gaps, feasibility/ direction of assessment	**PED Report**	Internal trustee document	Optional	Optional
Assessment	Assessment Plan **Coordinator and Solicitor**	Plan of technical and analytical studies for the assessment: determine and quantify injury and determine damages	**Assessment Plan** (draft and final)	**State Director** Approval of assessment plan (i.e. BLM technical approach)	Y	Y

Rel. 1-1712
05/27/2008

Assessment	Restoration and Compensation Determination Plan (RCDP) **Coordinator w/ Economist and Solicitor**	Description of methods to determine damages claim, using early data, assessment results	Detailed determination of damages for restoring injured resources, lost services	**State Director** Approval of methodology to be used; w/AP, Report of Assessment, or stand alone doc	Y	Y
Assessment	Report of Assessment **Coordinator and Solicitor**	Report to public of assessment results: restoration needs, damages	Report of Assessment (draft and final) with attachments	**State Director** Approval of Assessment conclusions	Y	Y
Post Assessment	Damages Claim **Coordinator and Solicitor, Economist and staff**	Compilation of prioritized restoration action costs + past and future trustee costs	Document with attachments (final Report of Assessment, etc)	**State Director** Approval of BLM Damages Claim for negotiations		
Post Assessment	Settlement Position **Solicitor w/ Coordinator, Economist / staff**	BLM terms acceptable for settlement	Agreement in Principle or Consent Decree, letter of concurrence	**State Director** Approval of BLM settlement terms. Solicitor letter to DOJ recommending entry of settlement.	Y	
Post Assessment	Restoration Plan **Coordinator and Staff, Economist, w/ Solicitor**	Plan Restoration Actions, post claim receipt, compliance with NEPA	Restoration Plan (draft and final)	**State Director** Which restoration actions to implement	Y	Y

X: Indicates party should receive document
Y: Indicates party should be invited to review and comment on document

2.1.3　DOI Lead for NRDAR: The Authorized Official

Every DOI NRDAR case must have a designated Authorized Official (AO) from among the bureaus involved in that case. If a bureau conducts a case alone it must still request and receive AO designation. The Secretary of the Interior has delegated the AO role to the directors of the resource-managing bureaus.

The AO is the administrative lead of DOI NRDAR efforts on a particular case. The AO represents all of the Secretary's trusteeship interests, in close consultation with the respective managers of the involved bureaus. The AO for a case is responsible for the conduct of the NRDAR. This includes the organization, coordination, communication, and administration of the case and the trustee council. These duties supporting the function of the trustee council begin as soon as the BLM and other agencies begin evaluating whether and how to proceed with NRDAR, thus the designation process should commence very early in the case. If several DOI bureaus are involved in a case, their respective staff and managers are engaged in case activities. The AO is responsible for approving decisions to proceed with NRDAR and for signing process documents such as the notice of intent to proceed, the Assessment Plan (AP), and the restoration plan. All critical documents in a case require the AO signature, with prior concurrences from the other involved bureaus; if an NRDAR document is not signed by the officially designated AO, the validity of the document may be challenged.

Since the NRDAR process is a legal process, it is imperative that an AO or AO staff work closely with an attorney from the Office of the Solicitor at the inception of a NRDAR case. The AO assists and supports the Office of the

Solicitor and the Department of Justice in representing the Department's interests in any discussions and/or negotiations or litigation involving NRDAR claim development or NRDAR claim resolution with PRPs.

2.1.4 Authorized Official Designation

When a DOI bureau requests AO designation, it sends a request to the DOI Restoration Program Office staff, which sends notices to the BLM and other bureaus. The AO designation request formally invites the BLM to evaluate whether it has resource interests at the site and wishes to become involved in the case, and whether the BLM concurs with the requesting bureau being the AO, or wishes to request AO designation itself. The BLM may respond to the DOI AO designation process in the following ways:

- ◆ If the BLM has no resource interests or declines to be involved, a BLM staff person from the State Office may provide response to the DOI of this BLM decision.

- ◆ If the BLM decides that it is affected at the site and wishes to be involved, a BLM staff person provides informal response to DOI, and then DOI sends a formal request to the State Director. The State Director then indicates to DOI the BLM intention to be involved and the BLM position regarding the AO designation request.

In 2001, the BLM Director delegated to the State Directors the authority to make all BLM case decisions, concur with AO designation requests made by other bureaus, and act as the AO for DOI. The FWS, BIA, USBR, and NPS have delegated these authorities to their Regional Directors. Each bureau's managing authority for other NRDAR case activities is similarly at the AO level, as per DOI Manual 521.

2.1.5 The BLM and the Authorized Official

The BLM State Director may wish, or may be requested, to be the AO for a case. The State Director should weigh the significance of BLM resource interests at the site, relative to those being considered by other trustee agencies, when considering AO designation. Typically the bureau with the greatest resource interests at a site takes on the AO role. The State Director also should weigh the administrative leadership and staff availability and capability that the BLM can dedicate to the case. Other bureaus involved in the case will continue to act on behalf of their trusteeship interests. If a BLM State Director wishes to be delegated as the DOI AO for a specific case, the Coordinator may make the request for designation to the DOI. The Coordinator should contact the National Operations Center (NOC), Division of Science and Resource Services, or Washington Office (WO) for assistance with the AO request.

If the BLM is the AO for a case, the day-to-day coordination and administrative responsibilities are carried out by the BLM Coordinator, serving as the case manager for the involved DOI bureaus.

If the BLM is the DOI AO, the BLM also may receive designation by the other involved Federal trustees to act as the Federal LAT. If the case involves State and/or tribal trustees, the DOI AO could be designated as the LAT for all agencies in the case. Additional information regarding the AO roles and responsibilities is available from the NOC, as well as in technical references and other NRDAR guidance documents.

2.1.6 Deciding To Proceed with NRDAR

The BLM may decide to proceed with NRDAR activities to characterize or implement the actions needed to restore injured BLM-managed resources or service losses at a site. The path of this decision process may differ, depending on whether or not the BLM is in charge of some or all of the response activities, and takes or considers removal actions. Note that there must be a viable and liable PRP in order for the BLM to recover assessment costs and obtain funds to conduct restoration.

2.1.6.1 BLM Response Sites

As the response agency at a site, the BLM conducts natural resource injury scoping, along with its removal site evaluation, according to policy. If significant resource injury concerns remain after the removal actions, the BLM may decide to conduct NRDAR activities because the restoration needs are not evident or the restoration is not achieved within the removal actions. In such cases, the Coordinator should alert the Field Office Manager, who should recommend to the State Director that NRDAR activities may be necessary. These NRDAR activities may inform the BLM of the restoration actions that the BLM should take, or that the PRP should fund or implement. Post-removal NRDAR activities would typically coincide with the remedial process. If the BLM considers NRDAR activities, the Coordinator should notify the DOI and inform other potentially interested bureaus and agencies so that they can determine if they have resource interests. If the BLM wishes to lead the NRDAR process, the State Director should request AO designation from DOI.

2.1.6.2 Non-BLM Response Sites

The BLM may decide to conduct NRDAR activities at sites where the BLM receives notification of releases or spills potentially affecting the BLM-managed land or resources. The State Office normally receives notification from the DOI in an AO designation request; the BLM staff may already be participating with other bureaus at some sites in response activities or preliminary NRDAR activities. The BLM may learn of a prospective NRDAR site directly from a response agency like EPA or through the DOI. Upon receiving notification, the Field Office or State Office should designate a Coordinator to evaluate the BLM interests at the site. The Field Office Manager familiar with the site should decide whether the BLM should conduct NRDAR activities, and if so, make a recommendation to the State Director.

2.2　THE TRUSTEE COUNCIL, THE AO, AND LEAD ADMINISTRATIVE TRUSTEE

NRDAR activities for a specific site often involve two or more agencies, each acting on its authorities as a natural resource trustee. In these situations, the agencies should form a trustee council and promptly prepare a mutually agreed upon MOU. The MOU should include a confidentiality agreement requiring the signatory agencies to hold as confidential (i.e., protect) the data and information they jointly or individually generate from outside disclosure. This confidentiality agreement could include response agencies and PRPs with whom the trustees have a cooperative agreement.

The managers of the involved agencies are the formal members of the trustee council; they usually have staff representatives who regularly attend council meetings as well as legal representation by the Office of the Solicitor. The trustee council is the decision-making forum for the case. For cases involving only DOI bureaus, the leadership of the council is the DOI AO. When a case also involves agencies outside DOI, the council designates the LAT to lead the council. The AO for the DOI and the LAT for the entire council provide overall administrative support and represent the council to the public and other outside entities. The AO or the LAT is the final signor of case documents, with the concurrence of the other agency managers. Regardless of which agency acts as the AO or the LAT, all involved agency managers retain their full agency authorities and prerogatives.

2.3　MANAGEMENT INVOLVEMENT AND DECISIONS

This section identifies the specific process steps and points at which a BLM State Director and District/Field Office Manager should provide BLM approval or make decisions on behalf of BLM trusteeship interests for a case. These are all of the process steps that would happen if the NRDAR activities for that case follow the entire regulatory process. The preparation of documents and NRDAR activities supporting these process steps may be carried out by State Office staff or District/Field Office staff, acting as the Coordinator or case manager for the NRDAR case, or in support of the Coordinator. The steps and decision points fall into the following categories:

♦ Administrative steps related to organization and coordination (see Section 2.3.1);

♦ Technical steps related to the scientific process and documentation of the case (see Section 2.3.2); and

♦ Legal steps related to communications and rapport with the PRPs (see Section 2.3.3).

2.3.1　State Director: Administrative Process Approvals and Decision Points

♦ **Determination to participate as an affected bureau on an NRDAR case.**
The State Director provides a formal response to a DOI request for BLM concurrence on an AO designation if the BLM decides to participate in a case as an "affected" bureau. The initial coordination of this request should

be conducted by BLM State/Field Office staff and the case Coordinator. The staff or Coordinator normally provide an informal response of the BLM determination to the DOI prior to the DOI request for formal response from the State Director. If the BLM determines that it is not an "affected" bureau, a State Office staff person may provide such response to the DOI.

♦ **Concurrence in AO designation requests.**
If the BLM is an "affected" bureau, the State Director provides written concurrence or non-concurrence with the requesting bureau's designation as the AO to the DOI. If the BLM is not an "affected" bureau, a State Office staff person may provide the BLM concurrence regarding the AO designation.

♦ **Request for BLM designation as the AO for NRDAR activities.**
The State Director requests to be designated as the DOI AO if BLM determines that it has important resource interests at the site, has staff to carry out the administrative responsibilities of the AO, and wishes to lead the involved DOI bureaus. The Coordinator should make the request to the DOI on behalf of the State Director. The Coordinator's request initiates the AO designation process.

♦ **Concurrence or signature on annual joint requests for case funding submitted to DOI.**
Annually, the State Director provides concurrence on joint NRDAR funding proposals involving BLM for cases in the State. In the late summer of each year, the case team submits funding requests or reports, along with bureau management and Office of the Solicitor concurrences prior to submitting the request to DOI. The State Director confirms the work that BLM and the other involved bureaus intend to do during the upcoming year on the case and the funds requested to carry it out. If BLM is the AO, the State Director requests concurrence from equivalent managers of the involved bureaus on the joint funding proposals, and then signs the funding requests for the case. This concurrence request should be sent by BLM State Office staff on behalf of the State Director.

♦ **Requests for concurrence from bureaus on case documents or decisions when the BLM is the AO.**
The State Director, when acting as the DOI Authorized Official, seeks concurrence from the other involved bureaus on case documents and decisions. The Coordinator should send concurrence requests to bureau managers on behalf of the State Director. The State Director should receive the other bureau manager concurrences before providing the AO signature representing all trusteeship interests of the DOI. Once the State Director makes the AO decision, copies of the decision document should be sent to the respective bureaus.

♦ **Allocation of State Office staff and fiscal resources to conduct NRDAR activities.**
The State Director determines which staff—the State Office or Field Office—should carry out case management and other case efforts, depending on the complexity of the case. The State Office staff may conduct these activities or act in support of Field Office staff. Funding to support this work may be available from the PRP, the DOI, or it may be obtained from appropriated funds.

♦ **Designation of Coordinator to evaluate BLM interests and conduct NRDAR activities.**
The State Director should ensure that a Coordinator is designated from the State Office or Field Office to evaluate whether the BLM wishes to be involved as an "affected" bureau for a prospective NRDAR case. NOC staff may be available to carry out duties of the Coordinator. The State Director should designate the Coordinator in conjunction with input from the Field Office Manager. Factors to consider include whether the BLM will act as the DOI AO and which office has the staff expertise needed to sufficiently conduct BLM NRDAR activities and coordinate with other agencies, as well as other factors.

2.3.2 State Director: Technical Process Approvals and Decision Points

♦ **PAS report indicating a BLM decision that NRDAR activity is warranted.**
Following the case team evaluation of key basic information for a site, the State Director concurs with the Pre-Assessment Screen report, if in agreement. The report documents the determination that the trustees are warranted to proceed with NRDAR activities and becomes the basis for commencing NRDAR.

◆ **Natural Resource Damage Assessment Plan (AP).**
The State Director concurs with the AP, which describes the trustees' intended methods to collect and analyze information to determine natural resource injuries and interim lost services, restoration needs, and the amount of damages. The Plan is reviewed publicly before it is finalized and implemented. It may be issued in parts and supplemented as the technical approach is refined or assessment plans substantially change. Substantial changes in direction from the original plan may necessitate a subsequent State Director concurrence and AO signature.

◆ **Restoration and Compensation Determination Plan (RCDP).**
The State Director concurs with this plan document, if in agreement. The plan may be released for public review with the AP, during the assessment process or with the Report of Assessment following the assessment process. If released on its own, the RCDP requires State Director concurrence and AO signature. The RCDP presents the process for determining the damages for the case. The RCDP identifies restoration alternatives, selects the preferred alternative, and describes how the trustees will determine the cost of implementing the selected alternative.

◆ **Report of Assessment and associated documents.**
The State Director concurs with this report, if in agreement. This report presents the findings and outcomes of the assessment, especially the restoration actions the trustees believe are necessary to sufficiently address injuries. It describes how the trustees made their determinations, which are the basis for the amount of natural resources damages that make up the claim. This document must be publicly reviewed.

◆ **BLM internal position, indicating the BLM claim regarding monetary damages.**
The State Director must approve the BLM monetary damages claim, including restoration costs and past and future BLM trustee costs, before it is presented in negotiations or used in litigation. The position is developed by the case team and Solicitor for management approval.

◆ **BLM Terms of Settlement and Trustees' Settlement**
The State Director must approve the settlement terms negotiated for the BLM and concur with the trustees' settlement. The settlement document may be an Agreement in Principle or subsequent consent decree, which is lodged in court. The prospective settlement may need to be briefed in the WO and the DOI prior to State Director acceptance for the BLM.

◆ **Restoration Plan describing the trustees' plan to restore using the monetary damages obtained**
The State Director approves and concurs with the issuance of the restoration plan, to ensure that BLM resources are adequately addressed in restoration. The Plan describes how the trustees will restore injured natural resources with the damages received. The Plan receives public review before it is finalized and implemented and, by DOI policy, is subject to NEPA. Plan implementation also may involve BLM commitments to conduct or oversee restoration actions, as well as to monitor restoration actions, as part of the trustee council.

2.3.3 State Director: Legal Process Approvals and Decision Points

These NRDAR process elements must be coordinated with the Solicitor; and where appropriate, the U.S. Department of Justice (DOJ).

◆ **Notice of Intent (NOI) letter sent to the potentially responsible parties inviting their cooperation.**
The State Director concurs with this letter, if in agreement. The letter is sent by the DOI Solicitor once the trustees have determined through the PAS that an NRDAR is warranted. It alerts the PRPs of the trustees' intention to proceed and conveys an invitation to the PRPs for cooperation.

◆ **Request to the Solicitor's Office to refer a damages claim to DOJ.**
The State Director concurs with this request, if in agreement. The request is made by the DOI Solicitor when the damages claim is prepared and approved, and DOJ involvement is necessary for negotiations or preparation for litigation.

- **Referral of a damages claim to DOJ.**
  The State Director concurs with this referral, if in agreement, for representation by DOJ in negotiations or preparation for litigation. The referral is based on the approved damages claim.

- **Notice of Intent (NOI) to sue the PRPs.**
  The State Director approves a letter, if in agreement, indicating the BLM intention to sue for natural resource damages. The DOI Solicitor or DOJ transmits the NOI to the responsible party. By taking this step, the BLM indicates that it is prepared for litigation.

- **Demand Letter to the PRPs presenting the BLM monetary damages.**
  The State Director concurs in any demand letter indicating BLM approval of the claim amount. The Solicitor transmits the demand letter to the PRPs.

- **Consent Decree: Records the mutually agreed settlement terms and is entered in court.**
  The State Director and all involved agencies must provide written concurrence and justification for the technical rationale to enter into any proposed settlement agreement or consent decree. The document is prepared by attorneys for the trustees and the PRPs. It contains the details of the agreement to settle the damages claim, including transfers of monetary damages or performance of work, schedules, and commitments by all parties involved in the settlement agreement. A covenant not to sue is usually included as part of any settlement agreement or consent decree.

- **Covenant Not To Sue (CNTS): Waives future rights to sue, except for unforeseen conditions.**
  The State Director approves and signs this document, if acceptable. Careful consideration should be given before approving a CNTS, because it indicates that BLM accepts the conditions and circumstances at the time and waives future legal recourse for natural resource damage claims against the specific PRPs, except for the development of new information about conditions and circumstances that would re-open the case.

2.3.4 District/Field Office Manager

District/Field Office Managers and staff may have important administrative and technical involvement for cases in their jurisdictions, even though the formal decisions regarding NRDAR activities are at the State Director level. These include the following:

- **Designation of Coordinator to evaluate the BLM interests at prospective NRDAR sites.**
  In conjunction with the State Director, the Field Office Manager should ensure that a Coordinator is designated from the State Office or Field Office to evaluate whether the BLM wishes to be involved as an "affected" bureau for a prospective NRDAR case. If so, the Field Office Manager may need to designate a Coordinator for the case. Factors to consider are whether the BLM will act as the DOI AO, which office has the staff expertise needed to sufficiently conduct BLM NRDAR activities and coordinate with other agencies, and other factors.

- **Verification of natural resource injury scoping completion at removal action sites.**
  The Field Office Manager approves the Action Memorandum for site-specific removal actions based on the RSE. This evaluation incorporates the findings of injury scoping per the CERCLA Response Handbook. At the conclusion of injury scoping, the BLM Coordinator completes the Injury Scoping Report and includes it in the Site Evaluation Report for the site. The Injury Scoping Report documents whether natural resource injuries have been identified so that restoration needs are considered and incorporated into the response actions, if possible.

- **Determination to initiate the BLM NRDAR activities after natural resource injury scoping.**
  The Field Office Manager recommends to the State Director whether to proceed to the Pre-Assessment Screen phase based on the results of natural resource injury scoping. If the restoration needed at a site is not accomplished by removal actions or the needs are not known in the available time, the Field Office Manager may determine to proceed to further NRDAR steps.

♦ **Allocation of staff and fiscal resources to conduct NRDAR activities.**
The Field Office Manager should endeavor to approve commitments of Field Office staff and resources needed to carry out NRDAR tasks, in coordination with staff from the State Office, the National Operations Center (NOC), and other trustee agencies. Note that in some cases, the District or Field Office staff may carry out NRDAR tasks and prepare documents for the State Director (see Sections 2.3.1, 2.3.2, and 2.3.3). Funding for this work may be available from the PRP, the DOI, or appropriated funds.

♦ **Routine oversight of the implementation of NRDAR technical activities.**
The Field Office Manager may regularly oversee NRDAR work at a site in the Field Office jurisdiction and advise the State Director on the conduct of tasks and other aspects of ongoing case activities.

2.4   STAFF NRDAR RESPONSIBILITIES

2.4.1   NRDAR Involved Staff

Staff from Field Offices and State Offices may have incidental or substantial roles in natural resource injury scoping and NRDAR activities at a site by supporting the Coordinator who conducts, coordinates, or oversees the BLM activities. Staff may be resource specialists from across the spectrum of program areas associated with the case, budget analysts, and others. The Coordinator should seek to involve all resources staff who may contribute to the BLM efforts to determine damages claims.

2.4.2   The BLM Coordinator

The BLM Coordinator is the staff person who conducts or leads site-specific pre-NRDAR and NRDAR activities regarding BLM-managed lands and resources. The BLM Coordinator represents the BLM State Director and Field Office Manager on case matters and may be at the State or Field Office level. The BLM Coordinator should have open communication with the BLM managers and the Solicitor regarding the case. The BLM Coordinator also may function as the BLM lead for response activities at the site, either for CERCLA hazardous substance releases or for oil spills that affect BLM-managed land. The BLM CERCLA Response Actions Handbook lists the response functions of the BLM Coordinator. The BLM Coordinator's role for NRDAR activities is sometimes called that of the case manager.

The BLM NRDAR activities on or regarding the BLM-managed lands often involve other agencies acting as co-trustees. Henceforth, any reference in this Handbook to the role, duties or responsibilities of "the Coordinator" is meant to indicate the BLM Coordinator working in cooperation and collaboration with staff representatives of the co-trustee agencies, as it deems appropriate for resource interests.

2.4.2.1 Notification

Coincident with the initiation of response activities after site verification, the Coordinator should notify the State Office and the BLM NOC of the beginning of injury scoping. The Coordinator should again notify the State Office and the NOC if further BLM NRDAR activities are contemplated. If BLM NRDAR activities are contemplated, the Coordinator must notify the DOI REO, who provides official notification to the other potentially affected DOI bureaus. The Coordinator also should consider directly notifying other trustee agencies of the prospective NRDAR activities for the site, particularly if a pre-NRDAR plan or agreement identifies co-trustee partnerships.

2.4.2.2 Technical responsibilities

The Coordinator's NRDAR-related tasks may begin with site verification and continue through the completion of restoration at a site. To begin NRDAR activities, the Coordinator should carry out the process of natural resource injury scoping during the time that the response RSE is underway. Injury scoping activities are described in Section 3.3. Depending on the results of injury scoping, the Coordinator should consider further NRDAR activities for the site using the Pre-Assessment screening process.

If the Coordinator finds that further NRDAR activities are warranted and the Field Office Manager determines that the BLM should continue NRDAR, the Coordinator should prepare to conduct the NRDAR process (see Section 3), including study and analysis planning, and field data collection, analysis, and interpretation. The Coordinator should seek assistance from the BLM staff in various disciplines regarding specific resources and administrative functions, and may obtain assistance from the NOC. Resource-specific assistance also may be available from staff of the co-trustee agencies when working on cooperative NRDAR cases.

2.4.2.3 Administrative responsibilities

The Coordinator should use project management principles and applicable tools to manage the NRDAR activities. The extent of the Coordinator's technical and administrative responsibilities depends on factors such as the complexity of the NRDAR case and the amount of administrative effort needed. If other agencies are involved in the case, the Coordinator may conduct some of these responsibilities (e.g., coordination and administrative tasks, such as document production, case documentation, financial management, and cost tracking) cooperatively with staff from the other involved agencies. If a NRDAR case involves co-trustees, the trustee council designates a case manager, usually within the same bureau as the DOI AO, who ensures that these responsibilities are carried out for the overall case. When a case also involves agencies outside DOI, the trustee council designates a lead agency, known as the LAT, to carry out these responsibilities. These roles are memorialized in the trustee MOU for the case. On complex cases, the administrative responsibilities of the BLM Coordinator may be extensive and this may limit or prevent primary involvement in specific technical activities.

The Coordinator should ensure that the following administrative responsibilities are carried out on behalf of the case:

- Coordinating with co-trustees and Federal, State, and local response agencies
- Seeking and acquiring funds for the case
- Ensuring that the case NRDAR activities are consistent with regulations
- Tracking and recording the costs of the NRDAR activities
- Maintaining the case file and Administrative Record (AR)
- Preparing the required documentation
- Issuing required notifications to other agencies and the PRP
- Publishing required notices
- Responding to comments
- Preparing claims or demands

The Coordinator may undertake the following general kinds of technical tasks in carrying out NRDAR-related activities:

- Assistance in the verification of sites for CERCLA hazardous substance releases or oil spills
- Ephemeral data collection and documentation
- Natural resource injury scoping in conjunction with removal site evaluations
- Assistance with verification of a viable PRP to pay for restoration
- Pre-Assessment evaluations of sites as prospective NRDAR cases
- Natural resource damage assessment planning
- Assessment implementation, including field and laboratory data collection, data analysis and management to support injury determinations, restoration scoping, and damages determination
- Restoration planning and implementation
- Assurance that all NRDAR activities taken are consistent with CERCLA or OPA

2.4.3 Legal Representation

It is important to recognize that NRDAR cases involve legal issues, determinations, analyses, and legal representation to resolve damages claims and recover NRDAR costs. NRDAR activities are "cases" because they result in legal actions, either a court-sanctioned consent decree or a civil lawsuit. The DOI Office of the Solicitor represents the interests of the BLM on all matters of law regarding BLM NRDAR activities, and provides advice on all legal matters regarding the case. If the State Director is the Authorized Official, the Coordinator, on behalf of the State Director, should request that the Regional Solicitor assign a DOI attorney to become the case attorney, as soon as it becomes apparent that NRDAR activities—such as initiation of the PAS—should begin. The Solicitor's Office is responsible for contacting DOJ and requesting an attorney be assigned to the case. DOJ represents the DOI in litigation matters, including negotiations and litigation on NRDAR matters. The Solicitor's Office together with agency representatives, work cooperatively with DOJ in NRDAR case development. The Solicitor's Office attorney is considered agency counsel for the case and should be a formal member of the trustee council and be kept involved in all case developments. Some cases involve criminal matters that require the collection of evidence and law enforcement expertise. Settlement agreements and consent decrees are filed with a U.S. District Court, which provides resolution of NRDAR claims.

2.4.4 Other BLM Staff

The Coordinator should seek assistance from BLM budget and finance staff, administrative specialists, and other appropriate resource specialists, commensurate with the administrative and technical needs of the NRDAR case. The Coordinator should periodically evaluate the case workload to ensure that sufficient staff resources are available. If the case requires extensive administrative effort or the assessment activities are complicated, the Coordinator should consider dedicated assistance to oversee one of these functions. Case funding may be used for all staff working specifically on case matters. The NOC is available to provide assistance and expertise in all aspects of NRDAR activities.

Trustee councils, composed of representatives of the affected agencies, provide official and organized forums to manage cases, and many case tasks may be shared. Contractors in the United States that are skilled and experienced in all facets of NRDAR work are available through the BLM response contractor, the General Services Administration (GSA), or contracting mechanisms of other trustees.

Where to go for Help within the DOI

1. **The Division of Resource Services (DSRS)** of the BLM National Operations Center (NOC) in Denver, Colorado has senior technical expertise in NRDAR program and process implementation, the CERCLA and OPA response process, and related areas of technical support.

2. **The Washington Office Resource Programs in WO200** may provide assistance with program, policy, or resource issues, and provide staff contacts or technical references.

3. **The DOI Restoration Program Office and Work Group** provide advice and recommendations on issues related to the DOI NRDAR authorities, responsibilities, and implementation of the natural resource damage provisions of CERCLA, OPA, and CWA. The BLM has a representative in the Work Group. See http://restoration.doi.gov/.

4. **The Office of the Solicitor** has eight regional and six branch offices that assign NRDAR case attorneys. A Regional Solicitor heads each regional office and an Associate Regional Solicitor heads each branch office. See http://www.doi.gov/sol/organizations/regions/main.htm for current contact information. Also, the Branch of Environmental Restoration under the Division of Parks and Wildlife in the Washington Office provides assistance on programmatic issues.

5. **The DOI Office of Program Policy Analysis in the Office of the Secretary** has economists with extensive NRDAR experience, particularly regarding the use of Habitat and Resource Equivalency Analysis and other assessment. See http://www.doi.gov/ppa.

2.4.5 Case File and Administrative Record (AR)

The case file is a file or collection of files that generally contains all NRDAR decision documents, objective communications, reports, and other documents related to a case. The AR is a subset of the case file and contains the specific communications, reports, and other documents that the trustees use to make case decisions and select the actions they carry out for the case.

2.4.5.1 Case File

The Coordinator must develop and maintain a case file for the NRDAR case. The case file should be established when injury scoping is completed if the Coordinator determines that removal actions will not sufficiently address restoration needs and NRDAR activities are contemplated. The case file includes all objective materials that pertain to the case, from its beginning to its conclusion. Such materials include meeting reports and minutes, informational reports, articles, data, and photographs. The case file can include privileged and confidential documents. The Coordinator should ensure the completeness of the case file by including all relevant BLM staff contributions to NRDAR activities. In addition, if the BLM maintains the case file for a multi-agency trustee council, the Coordinator should ensure that all documentation of the BLM NRDAR activities is included in the case file. The NRDAR case file should be kept separate from the response action case file, although the files may contain many documents in common.

2.4.5.2 Administrative Record

The Coordinator also should begin to assemble an AR at the conclusion of the PAS Report to facilitate public involvement and support eventual cost recovery. A single AR covering all involved agency activities may be maintained for the entire case. The AR also provides defensible evidence that the trustees have conducted the assessment properly. The AR should include all documents and materials the trustee agencies rely upon or consider in the decision-making process, such as the decision to pursue NRDAR, determination and quantification of injury, and/or selection of restoration actions. Examples include reports, policies, guidelines, factual information and data, communications, notes, and decision documents. The Coordinator should include all such documents, even if they are not ultimately used in the decisions or reflect negatively on decisions made by the trustees. The AR may include references and Internet links to relevant documents. Check with the case Solicitor regarding AR contents.

Contents of an Administrative Record

The following NRDAR documents are appropriate for the AR. Check with the case Solicitor regarding specific contents.

- Resource-related site description documents
- Injury Scoping Report with supporting documents
- Designation of DOI AO documents
- Designation of LAT documents
- Inter-trustee MOU
- Confidentiality Agreement
- PAS with supporting documents
- "Notice of Intent" letter with PRP identified and supporting documents
- Trustee - PRP MOU
- Draft and final AP with supporting documents
- Public/PRP comments on AP
- PED with supporting documents
- Injury determination and quantification documents
- Damages determination documents
- Legal documents supporting NRDA case
- RCDP with supporting documents
- Draft and final Report of Assessment with supporting documents
- Public/PRP comments on Report of Assessment
- Case settlement consent decree with supporting documents
- Restoration Plan with NEPA documentation and supporting documents
- Public/PRP comments on Restoration Plan
- Restoration Action Plans and contracts with supporting documents
- Restoration Completion Reports
- Restoration action monitoring documents

The AR includes documents that may be "privileged" and contain protected information. Once the AR is complete, privileged information is redacted from the record. However, the index of the record must identify these documents and indicate why they are being withheld. The AR can be organized in chronological order or by topic. An index containing document identification numbers and descriptions is prepared so that documents can be readily located. Public reading rooms often are established at local libraries or community centers to allow the public access to the AR.

The NRDAR guidance under CERCLA does not specify when to open an AR. Under CERCLA, the decision to assemble the AR should be made with input from the Solicitor and may depend on when the trustee council releases NRDAR documents to the public and the PRPs. The Coordinator should consider opening an AR when the trustees determine to conduct a formal NRDAR.

The NRDAR guidance under OPA specifies that an AR is mandatory at the initiation of a NRDAR case. Under OPA there are two types of ARs: (1) one opened at the initiation of the restoration planning process (15 CFR §990.45); and (2) one opened at the beginning of restoration implementation (15 CFR §990.61).

The Coordinator should maintain the AR in a manner consistent with the Administrative Procedures Act (5 U.S.C. 550-59, 701-06). The AR made available to the public should not contain original documents, especially correspondence. The AR should be kept near the site and accessible to the public.

2.5   NRDAR Case Financial Management

This section contains information regarding financial management for specific NRDAR cases. The Coordinator or case manager should be primarily responsible for these tasks, but other staff with budget-keeping and accounting expertise may be required, depending on the financial complexity of the activities.

2.5.1   Funding

2.5.1.1 CERCLA NRDAR Funds

For CERCLA release sites, the Coordinator should anticipate that the BLM bears the costs of injury scoping and Pre-Assessment screening through the normal budget process of the BLM. Limited NRDAR funds may be available as BLM discretionary funds through the BLM Work Group member (see Section 2.1.1) for exploratory NRDAR activities at new BLM sites.

If the BLM decides to conduct further NRDAR activities, funding may be available from the DOI Restoration Fund. DOI allocates case funds through an annual proposal process, based on case merit and DOI preparedness to carry out planned assessment activities. The DOI Program Office reviews case proposals in the fall and disburses funds in mid-winter. For cases involving two or more bureaus, DOI requires joint funding requests.

The DOI Restoration Fund allocates funding in three categories:

1. Feasibility: One-time allocation for prospective cases needing to finalize determinations that a case is warranted;

2. Initial: To initiate warranted cases and begin to coordinate the assessment process; and

3. Ongoing: Annual allocations to continue cases as they proceed through the assessment process toward recovering damages claims.

NRDAR cases receive DOI funds annually as long as they are progressing effectively toward assessment and restoration goals. DOI allocates two main categories of ongoing funds: (1) overall administrative case management; and (2) the planning and conducting or contracting of technical studies, analyses, and reports. Case assessments typically take two or more years to plan and implement; thus, the funds cases receive are on a "no year" basis, and the case funds allocated to the BLM are not subject to the BLM carry-over rules. If the case proposal receives funding, the DOI NRD Program Office will allocate the funds to the individual bureaus, and the BLM will receive its share of the case allocations in January or February. Once the DOI transfers the funds to the BLM, and the WO budget officer transfers the funds to the State, the State or Field Office budget officer should adjust the case-specific spending target to reflect the annual allocation.

The Coordinator should assemble the BLM anticipated case costs during the spring and summer, prior to the DOI funding proposal due date in late August. NRDAR case budgeting is on a calendar year basis, because of the funding allocation schedule. This should include both case management and technical study/analysis costs for all involved staff and management of the BLM. The Coordinator should plan BLM case spending needs in close coordination with trustee council representatives of the other involved DOI bureaus.

To request funding from the DOI Restoration Fund, the Coordinator should begin the process in late spring. Completing the proposal may require a number of weeks and coordinating form completion with other bureaus may require additional time.

The Coordinator should do the following to initiate the fund request process:

1. Verify the site, complete natural resource injury scoping (see Section 3.3), and evaluate site conditions using the PAS criteria (see Section 3.4.2);

2. Identify the PRP (e.g., share PRP search efforts and information with response activities);

3. Make Notifications for Cooperation, Coordination, and Assistance in Case Development;

4. Contact other BLM staff with expertise in resource programs potentially affected at the site;

5. Contact the State Office Program Lead;

6. Alert other bureau, Federal, State, and tribal counterparts with resource interests; invite their involvement;

7. Contact NOC NRDAR program staff and WO for help; send NRIS Report with supporting information;

8. Contact the Regional Solicitor to obtain legal assistance;

9. Prepare the funding proposal, including administrative, scientific and technical, and legal assistance costs;

10. Obtain the State Director's signature. For joint bureaus proposals, obtain concurrences of other managers.

2.5.1.2 OPA NRDAR Funds

For OPA incidents, the BLM may provide funding to conduct response, NRDAR activities, and restoration. Funds are normally available from the U.S Coast Guard National Pollution Fund Center (NPFC) to conduct response and emergency restoration activities, and initiate NRDAR activities. The NPFC allocates funds for oil spill response in response to agencies submitting a Pollution Removal Funding Agreement (PRFA) for the incident. For NRDAR activities, the NPFC promptly approves spending authority for emergency restoration; it approves interagency agreements to fund the initiation of NRDAR activities on a reimbursable basis, in response to receiving an NRDAR Initiate Request. As soon as the early NRDAR tasks are known, the BLM should prepare or contribute to an Initiate Request to obtain funding to start NRDAR Pre-Assessment activities. Initiate Requests should be coordinated among the involved DOI bureaus, and submitted by the AO bureau. It is important not to mix response and NRDAR activities and funding sources. Funds for subsequent OPA restoration planning are available from the NPFC, also on a reimbursable basis, through an interagency agreement (IAG) that describes the specific work and itemized costs. The use of all NPFC funds requires careful cost tracking. The NPFC also may fund the ultimate restoration actions on a reimbursable basis, if PRP funding is unavailable or their costs have exceeded established limits of liability. Contact the NPFC for more information at http://www.uscg.mil/hq/npfc/. It may be possible to negotiate for PRP funding to support the initial NRDAR activities until NPFC spending authority is obtained.

2.5.2 Cost Coding

For NRDAR activities supported by DOI funding, the Coordinator should use Sub-Activity 9210. The Coordinator also may use funding from BLM appropriations in other Sub-Activities such as 1640 or 1010, if available. For any

NRDAR activities funded by PRPs or sources other than the BLM and DOI, the Coordinator should use Sub-Activity 9260. Oil spill NRDAR activities using funds from the NPFC should also be coded to 9260. Examples include cooperative assessments and post-settlement restoration with related oversight activities funded by the damages received. Sub-Activity 9210 may not be used for post-settlement restoration. Funds from any of these Sub-Activities are equally cost-recoverable, and efforts must be made to avoid or recover NRDAR costs.

The Coordinator must establish a four-character alpha Special Interest Project Code (SIPC) for NRDAR, in accordance with the BLM financial system, with the assistance of the local budget officer, the Division of Business Services, and the Division of Resource Services. The Coordinator should establish the SIPC to distinguish NRDAR case spending as soon as discrete NRDAR activities begin (i.e., when the PAS process begins at the conclusion of injury scoping). The NRDAR SIPC consists of the State two-letter code, followed by Q, and then an alpha letter for the numerical order of initiation in the State. For example, the SPIC for the second case in Colorado would be COQB. The SIPC should apply to all funds used for NRDAR work on that specific case, and it should remain with the case throughout the duration of NRDAR activities. The NRDAR SIPC may be different from the project code established for the response process. The Program Elements pertaining to NRDAR are BF, HO, NP, NQ, and MG.

> **Program Elements**
>
> BF – Assess Hazmat or Oil Spill Sites
> HO – Restoration Implementation
> MG – Monitor and Maintain Hazmat and NRDAR Sites
> NP – Evaluate PRPs for Cost Recovery
> NQ – Process Hazmat and Oil Cost Recovery Cases

2.5.3 Cost Avoidance and Recovery

For the DOI and NPFC funds and all NRDAR activities, it is mandatory that the BLM make every effort to avoid incurring or recover costs. The Coordinator should seek a cooperative assessment with known PRPs to avoid incurring NRDAR costs, as long as the cooperative efforts sufficiently address BLM restoration needs. All reasonable NRDAR costs and the costs of restoration are recoverable. Each viable PRP whose releases caused resource injuries at a site can be liable for the BLM NRDAR assessment and restoration costs. The following costs are recoverable:

◆ Primary restoration, including planning the restoration, implementing the action, oversight and monitoring;

◆ Compensation (including compensatory restoration) for the replacement of lost services, including planning the actions, implementing the action, oversight, and monitoring; and

◆ All reasonable assessment activities, regardless of funding source, from injury scoping through the damage assessment process, including direct and indirect costs, and legal support for the assessment, unless contributed by the PRP or third party.

2.5.4 Cost Tracking and Documentation

Cost tracking and documentation should be a routine part of conducting NRDAR activities. The Coordinator should establish a cost documentation file to track case spending on NRDAR activities when it is evident that post-injury scoping NRDAR activities should begin. The cost documentation file is important for managing the case budget, as well as to facilitate the reporting of fund uses and provide documentation for cost recovery. The Coordinator should engage the assistance of budget and finance staff for cost documentation.

Normally, the Coordinator should track injury scoping costs within the response and PRP search activities. If injury scoping efforts accrue significant costs, it could be necessary to track them separately as well. Subsequent NRDAR costs should be tracked separately from response or remedial action cost. Ultimately, all of these cost documentation files may be used in establishing the damage claim. The costs of restoration may be in addition to, and different from, response costs for which the PRP also may be held responsible. Recovery of costs is discussed further in Section 3.

The cost documentation file should be a subpart of the overall case file. It should be maintained with the case file but kept separate from the AR. The cost documentation file should contain hard copies of the relevant documents and should not rely on electronic data files.

NRDAR costs typically include labor, travel, supplies, equipment, field and laboratory investigations, sampling, analytical testing, data analysis and interpretation, report preparation, evaluation of restoration alternatives, public outreach requirements, and contractor support. All staff contributing to BLM NRDAR efforts should code labor, travel, and other costs to the case-specific codes, and keep records of their case-related costs, according to the funds allocated for those efforts. The Coordinator should compile the names of the BLM personnel working on the case, organizational codes, pay grades, hours worked, and NRDAR activities performed, as well as travel costs by person, and all other operational costs (e.g., equipment and contracts). Cost documentation records should include both direct and indirect costs (e.g., agency overhead costs).

For cost recovery in some cases, the official BLM financial records may need to be supplemented by "cuff records" that further describe actual activities and costs, including separate forms for listing labor, travel, and operations spending. Appendix B contains example "cuff records" that may be used for this purpose. The Coordinator should evaluate whether these forms are necessary to document case costs for recovery.

Once a case begins receiving funds from the DOI Restoration Program through the annual process, the Coordinator provides a description of the use of the funds to DOI in subsequent annual proposals. The DOI Restoration Program incorporates the information into a database of NRDAR financial information.

Cost documentation for a case should include the following:

1. Management Information Systems (MIS) records for offices with staff working on the case. The records should pertain to the case and be identified by SIPC, Sub-activity, and Program Element.
2. Employee timesheets for each employee involved. On the timesheets, the work on the case is distinguished by the Sub-activity, SIPC, and Program Element. Cuff records may be needed; examples of cuff record needs include efforts to provide additional records to support contentious cost recovery, to record work activities over an extended time period, or to track large or complicated case costs.
3. Travel vouchers for each employee involved. Travel vouchers must be supported by evidence of invoice payments for purchases of lodging and transportation.
4. Contracts and purchase orders for contract work, equipment, and supplies, supported by evidence of payments for all invoices and purchases charged on the case.

---

3. THE NRDAR PROCESS

3.1 OVERVIEW

This section presents the basic functional elements of the entire NRDAR process. The process includes pre-NRDAR preparation, injury scoping, Pre-Assessment, assessment (including restoration planning and damages determination), and restoration implementation and other post-assessment activities. The full process has a number of specific NRDAR decision points, required documentation, and procedures for PRP and public review. The materials presented herein introduce Coordinators and staff to the regulatory approach for conducting efficient and practical NRDAR while fulfilling the BLM mission of maintaining the health of public land, restoring land that is harmed by misuse or accident, and preserving land uses.

NRDAR STEPS
◆ Pre-NRDAR Preparation
◆ Natural Resource Injury Scoping
◆ Pre-Assessment Screen
◆ Natural Resource Damage Assessment
▶   Assessment Plan
▶   Injury Determination
▶   Injury Quantification
▶   Damages Determination
◆ Post-Assessment

The NRDAR steps described in this section comprise a technically and administratively logical process to bring about restoration of injured BLM resources, document BLM decisions and actions, and involve the public, whose resources the BLM manages. The extent of the process that the Coordinator conducts will depend on site and case complexity, the availability of site data, the potential to reach agreements with PRPs that may preclude process elements, and other factors. The individual NRDAR steps described here may be brief and simplified or prolonged and extensive. Case planning should consider whether an expedited assessment may be possible, or a full NRDA may be necessary. The Coordinator should recognize that the course of the process may change with changes in technical information, response process developments, or trustee-PRP relationships.

3.2   Pre-Planning for NRDAR

NRDAR pre-planning activities, under both CERCLA and OPA, should prepare the BLM Coordinator to provide optimal reaction and response to NRDAR cases. Pre-planning activities include the following:

◆ Pre-arranging points of contact and communications among potentially involved agencies;

◆ Pre-arranging staff expertise and Agency resources that may be brought to bear at sites or incidents; and

◆ Training to ensure that NRDAR practitioners are familiar with NRDAR and its relationship to response actions.

The Coordinator[6] should refer to the BLM Field Office and State emergency response contingency plans for specific information that may be useful for injury scoping and NRDAR. Pre-planning may involve supplementing existing response contingency plans to include other trustee contact information, process steps to initiate NRDAR activities, and other relevant information. If possible, it should: identify NRDA expertise, area and regional response agencies and officials, and support services; establish notification systems; identify natural resources and services at risk; list potential sources of baseline information; list or reference existing regional and other restoration plans; provide sample documents for financial management and data management; and identify assessment funding issues and options. In addition, pre-NRDAR preparation may include identification of stakeholders who could be involved in a public review process. It may be possible to pre-identify possible sources of CERCLA releases and OPA oil spills on the basis of types of industries and authorized uses common in localities.

3.3   Natural Resource Injury Scoping (NRIS)

3.3.1 Purpose and Process

The purpose of Natural Resource Injury Scoping (NRIS) is to identify resource injuries and service losses to facilitate restoration within the removal action. Ideally, this scoping should be performed concurrently with the RSE. NRIS is especially applicable at BLM sites where the BLM may take the removal action. NRIS precedes the NRDAR process, and is not specifically prescribed in CERCLA or OPA regulations. NRIS involves an abbreviated assessment of resource injuries and service losses within the limited timeframe of the RSE. Although the RSE timeframe is typically shorter than a full assessment would require, it may be possible to characterize the injuries and losses sufficiently to identify specific restoration needs through coordinated efforts and data sharing with response activities. If the Coordinator can identify the site's restoration needs within that timeframe, it may be possible to integrate those actions into the removal actions. If the abbreviated assessment in NRIS does not result in identifying the restoration needs, and significant resource injuries or service losses have occurred, the Coordinator should consider further NRDAR activities.

A discovery or notification that an OPA oil spill or CERCLA hazardous substance release has occurred is a trigger for the Coordinator to conduct injury scoping, at the same time as the removal evaluation or similar process. The RSE identifies potential pathways by which hazardous substances may be transported and pose health risk or environmental impacts. During injury scoping, the Coordinator and other field staff collect information to identify natural resource exposure to oil or hazardous substances and any potential injuries.

---

6. As noted in Section 2.4.2 of this Handbook, the BLM Coordinator is the staff person who conducts or oversees NRDAR activities.

The Coordinator should evaluate potential ground water and surface water pathways; soil and sediment pathways; food chain pathways; and air pathways. Any of these pathways could lead to exposure and injury of natural resources. In addition, field staff should consider whether released hazardous substances could adversely affect habitat quality or quantity to the detriment of biota dependent on that habitat, regardless of whether the organisms are directly exposed to hazardous substances.

The steps of injury scoping are as follows:

1. **Identify Resource Injury**
    The Coordinator should consider all natural resources and site uses that are or should be present at the site. Although the BLM focuses primarily on surface water, sediments, soils and geologic resources, and biological resources, the BLM also may be concerned with ground water and air.

BLM can address injuries at abandoned mines through the NRDAR Process

2. **Identify Baseline Resource Condition**
    The Coordinator should collect information to determine the baseline conditions of the resources thought to be injured. Baseline is the resource condition that would exist without the CERCLA release or oil spill thought to have caused the injury.

3. **Quantify Injury – Difference from Baseline**
    The Coordinator should quantify the injuries to resources, compared to their baseline conditions. Quantifying injury means counting the number of lost or harmed resources, or determining percentages of lost or injured resources, compared to their baseline condition. Note that if the planned removal action is anticipated to cause additional resource injury or service loss, the Coordinator should count this injury or loss in the restoration actions that are recommended.

4. **Quantify Restoration – How Much Is Needed**
    The Coordinator should determine the amount of restoration (i.e., numbers or percentages of resources to be restored or replaced) as a function of the extent or quantity of injury found. The Coordinator should then identify the restoration actions needed to achieve the quantity of restoration goals deemed necessary to restore the injured resources to baseline.

5. **Recommend Restoration in Removal Planning**
    The Coordinator should recommend the restoration actions or goals as part of the response actions being planned in the RSE.

Consider the following examples of possible restoration goals for incorporation into the response action:

◆   Remove contaminated soils to restore baseline soil chemistry and ensure that soil biota, plants, and soil processes are not adversely affected by residual contamination above baseline concentrations.

◆   Re-grade, re-contour, and re-vegetate with native species to accelerate natural recovery after disturbance related to response actions.

◆   Accelerate the recovery of a habitat or ecosystem to baseline condition, rather than only to risk-free condition, by reestablishing, for example:

   ▶   The quantity and quality of surface water flow that was present before the release.

   ▶   The quantity (depth) and quality (nutrient cycling ability, nutrient availability, water holding capacity) of soil that was present before the release and response action.

   ▶   The plant community composition and structure that provided ecological services, such as habitat or food supply, or use services, such as grazing, before the release and response action.

> ▸ Components of the food chain that support fish and wildlife, such as macro-invertebrate communities essential to insectivorous fish and wildlife, and small mammal communities essential for raptors and carnivorous mammals.

> ▸ The physical habitat that might have been degraded because of injuries caused by the release. For example, if a release (or the response action) eliminated vegetation and subsequent soil erosion degraded stream bank stability and caused siltation of fish spawning habitat in a stream, the physical degradation could be restored to the baseline condition.

◆ Restore aquatic habitat through riparian vegetation planting or in-stream work to return system to baseline physical condition or better after response actions.

◆ Achieve the recovery of healthy land and resource uses, such as grazing services.

◆ Re-establish access to the recreational services provided by the public land.

◆ Re-establish access to commodity services provided by the public land (e.g., mineral resources, mined materials).

The Coordinator should always monitor the success of the response action to ensure that the implemented response actions achieve the restoration goals that were incorporated into the action plan, or recommend further restoration actions if they are necessary.

In addition to resource injuries, there also may be losses of services because of resource injury. Natural resources provide ecological and human use services. Ecological services include habitat, food chain, and other ecosystem functions. Human use services include hiking, fishing, birding, enjoyment of preserved areas, hunting, grazing, flood and erosion control, water supplies, minerals production, and other services. For the BLM, habitat services are often the predominant concern. Services may be reduced from baseline levels when the resources are injured – the amount of service loss is the reduction from baseline over

Stream eroding base of rock dump

the period of injury. It is important to identify the measure of service carefully, such as acres of bird nesting or fishery user days. The time period may be from the beginning of injured condition until the resources return to their baseline condition.

If a release or discharge is small, dilute, of short duration, rapidly contained, or quickly dispersed or diluted, the potential harm to natural resources might be limited and confined. In such cases, potential injuries to natural resources might be adequately addressed by a prompt removal action, with no additional action needed to restore resources and their services to baseline condition.

If the injury caused by the discharge or release is potentially more substantial, actions beyond removal may be necessary to restore resources or the services previously provided by the resources. The timing and nature of the response action will affect the extent and duration of continuing injuries to natural resources. In general, a less protective response action could result in greater residual injury to natural resources and a longer time period during which resource services are lost. This would lead to a more extensive restoration to return the resources to baseline condition and more compensation to replace the services the public has lost.

Estimating injury and restoration needs.

For some case situations, it may not be possible to reach certainty on all resource injuries or quantities within the RSE timeframe. In such cases, reasonable estimates may suffice, depending on resource importance and the removal actions that are planned. The Coordinator may need to seek advice from the National Operations Center or other sources

---

For older sites, sites occupying large areas, or sites having multiple contaminants, early characterization of restoration needs may be difficult, and sufficient restoration planning may ultimately require NRDAR.

3.3.2 Emergency Restoration

The immediate steps that are taken to respond to a release or threat of release or a spill should protect public health and safety and minimize the injury, destruction, or loss of resources. The Coordinator should determine whether there is a need for emergency restoration (i.e., actions that must be taken immediately to protect resources from new or continuing injury). Such actions may be closely related to the intended results of emergency removal actions. If the response action does not sufficiently address natural resource injury, the Coordinator may determine to undertake emergency restoration actions to address natural resource injury. Examples include actions that block a contaminant pathway or protect resources from imminent or continuing exposure. If a response agency is in charge of the site, the Coordinator must receive concurrence from that agency for the emergency restoration.

3.3.3 Ephemeral Data Collection

The Coordinator or field staff should be prepared to collect ephemeral data whenever they visit a site, while following the site entry policy and maintaining worker safety. Ephemeral data may be critical to understanding and documenting critical information about the release or the incident, and may be the most informative data ever available for the site. Discovering and collecting ephemeral information about the contamination or its effects might be possible only in the hours, days, or weeks immediately following the release. Compilation of such ephemeral information can be useful for planning response and restoration actions, and for determining whether NRDAR actions are needed. The Coordinator should ensure the quality of all record-keeping, data collection, sample integrity, chain of custody procedures, and other data quality measures undertaken during ephemeral data collection, so that the information is defensible if challenged.

3.3.4 Documentation

It is BLM policy to complete a NRIS Report form (see Appendix C) for all sites where a determination is made that a CERCLA release or an OPA oil spill has occurred and response actions may be warranted. The form reports whether injuries have been identified or are suspected as a result of a release of hazardous substances or an oil spill. The Coordinator should complete this report form to document the results of the NRIS process and that injury scoping has been accomplished at a site. If injuries have been identified or are suspected, the Coordinator should list the specific resources potentially injured and/or services lost. If specific injuries or losses are identified, the Coordinator should list the general restoration actions thought necessary, for recommendation in removal action planning. The Coordinator should list other agencies that do or may have resource interests at the site, and also list the known PRPs. This report should be completed and available for consideration during the removal preliminary assessment and in removal action planning.

The Field Office Manager and the Coordinator should sign the report to verify that the NRIS process has been completed for the site and that its results are available for response planning. The report should be placed in the case file and the AR. Supporting documentation regarding resource injuries and service losses and potential restoration actions should be attached to the NRIS Report and placed in the case file.

3.4   PRE-ASSESSMENT SCREEN

3.4.1 Purpose

The PAS is an evaluation process to discern whether NRDAR activities are warranted, with a reasonable probability of making a successful damages claim. A PAS is a rapid review of readily available information about the site, including the site history, the nature of the release or spill, the impacts of the release or spill on resources, and the identity of PRPs. The PAS identifies resources that are at risk of injury, describes transport pathways, and presents an estimate of areas where exposure and effects may have occurred.

Based on the NRIS findings and response actions taken, the Coordinator should determine whether to begin the PAS. If, during the NRIS process, the Coordinator determines that natural resource injuries may have occurred at a site and restoration may be necessary and that the response action does not sufficiently address injured resources or lost services, then the Coordinator should consider the evaluation process of the PAS.

The PAS includes notification, coordination, emergency actions, and evaluation of available data to determine whether NRDAR could and should be performed. At this point, the Coordinator should contact the Regional Office of the Solicitor to arrange for assignment of DOI legal counsel. If other agencies are involved at the site, the PAS phase should be conducted cooperatively. At the beginning of the PAS process, the Coordinator and the other involved DOI bureaus should begin the designation process for the DOI Authorized Official. If the Coordinator has completed NRIS, then the PAS criteria (see Section 3.4.2) may be answered.

For sites where the BLM is not the response agency but becomes aware of the potential of BLM resource injuries stemming from the release or spill, the PAS phase may be the first NRDAR activity the BLM conducts. During the PAS, the Coordinator should consider whether the BLM resources may require emergency restoration (see Section 3.3.2).

3.4.2   Pre-Assessment Screening Criteria

Both CERCLA and OPA regulations set criteria that the Coordinator should use in making the determination whether to proceed with NRDAR activities.

For either CERCLA hazardous substance releases or OPA spills, if the Coordinator, along with other involved trustees, determines that the criteria (listed in Section 3.4.2.1) have been met, then further NRDAR activities may be warranted based on the available information of site conditions.

For CERCLA sites, in addition to responding to the PAS criteria, the Coordinator should verify at least one liable and viable PRP. This element, although not part of the PAS process described in the regulations, is absolutely necessary for seeking natural resource damages under CERCLA to fund resource restoration and recover the damage assessment costs. Under OPA, it may be possible to fund restoration and recover assessment costs from the NPFC if a PRP is not identified, but trustees should make every effort to identify the PRP.

3.4.2.1 CERCLA PAS Criteria

The CERCLA NRDAR regulations instruct trustees to use five criteria to determine whether NRDAR activities are warranted at a site. Using available data, the Coordinator should determine whether:

◆ A discharge of oil or release of hazardous substances has occurred;

◆ The quantity and concentration of oil or hazardous substance released is sufficient that it potentially could cause harm to natural resources;

◆ Natural resources under management or control of the BLM potentially are adversely affected;

◆ Data sufficient to assess injuries, damages, and restoration needs are available or can be collected at reasonable cost; and

◆ Response actions will **not** adequately remedy the harm resulting from the release.

To help assess whether the available data are sufficient to show that injury has occurred or whether such data could be acquired with reasonable effort, the Coordinator should obtain the answer to the following questions:[7]

---

7. These questions should be revisited regularly during the NRDAR process, as the Coordinator builds the injury and damages case.

- Is the connection between the release and the potential injury clear?
- Are the degree, spatial extent, and temporal extent of the injury known or could they be defined with additional reasonable data collection, analysis, or interpretation?
- Are existing data of reliable quality?

3.4.2.2 OPA Criteria to Determine Jurisdiction and Restoration Planning

The OPA regulations describe a sequence of two sets of criteria for determining trustee jurisdiction for an incident and then whether to conduct restoration planning. Taken together, OPA criteria are similar to the release criteria. They are as follows:

(1) Jurisdiction (does the agency have trustee jurisdiction in the incident?)

- Has an incident occurred, as defined in 15 CFR §990.30;
- The incident is not:
  - Permitted under local, State, or Federal law;
  - From a public vessel, such as a military ship or other publicly owned facility; and
  - From an onshore facility subject to the Trans-Alaska Pipeline Authority Act.
- Natural resources under the trusteeship of the trustees may have been or may be injured as a result of the incident; and
- If jurisdiction is determined, then proceed to the second set of criteria.

(2) Restoration Planning (is it appropriate for the trustee to plan and implement restoration actions?)

- Injuries have resulted or are likely to result from the incident;
- Response actions will not address the injuries; and
- Feasible primary or compensatory restoration actions exist to address the potential injuries.

3.4.3 Review of Available Data

Because the purpose of the PAS is to determine whether assessment activities are warranted at a site, based on rapidly reviewing and documenting the site conditions, the PAS does not have to identify all injured resources, sources, pathways, nor PRPs who may have liability at the site. Data collected through the RSE, especially ephemeral data and other information collected in the NRIS, should be useful for the PAS and later assessment phases of NRDAR. Depending on the case timing and the site complexity, data collected during engineering evaluation/cost analysis (EE/CA) studies and other response investigations also can be useful for the PAS.

Other sources of data useful for the PAS include previously compiled baseline condition data; published literature, guidelines, and standards relevant to environmental toxicity or harm caused by oil, hazardous substances, or emergency response actions; documentation for planned or completed response actions; and documentation of similar incidents and resulting environmental effects. At sites where more complicated or lengthy actions, such as remedial investigations, ecological risk analyses, and feasibility studies have been undertaken by response agencies, a considerable amount of existing data and information could be very useful to the Pre-Assessment screening process.

3.4.4 Additional Data Collection for Pre-Assessment

Data collection prior to completion of the Pre-Assessment under CERCLA and OPA should be limited to the collection of ephemeral data and samples necessary to preserve perishable materials considered likely to have been affected by, and contain evidence of, the hazardous substance or oil. Such data may be available through the response process if the Coordinator determines that removal actions are insufficient and further site characterization is necessary for designing the response action.

3.4.5 Exemptions from NRDAR Liability

The Coordinator also should consider whether statutory exemptions from natural resource damages liability apply to the discharge or release. These considerations should involve legal advice from the Solicitor. A PRP may avoid natural resources damages liability if any of the following apply.

CERCLA Sections 107(f) (i) (j) and 114(c) exemptions:

♦ The harm resulting from the release was permitted and specifically identified as an irreversible and irretrievable commitment of natural resources in an environmental impact statement (EIS) or other comparable environmental analysis.

♦ The release and the entirety (the full extent and duration) of the harm caused by the release occurred before the enactment of CERCLA (December 1980).

♦ The release resulted from the legal application of a pesticide product registered under the Federal Insecticide, Fungicide, and Rodenticide Act (FIFRA) 7 U.S.C. 135-135k.

♦ The release resulted from a federally permitted release as defined in CERCLA Section 101 (10).

CWA Section 311(a) (2) and (b) (3) exemptions:

♦ Discharges in compliance with a National Pollutant Discharge Elimination System (NPDES) permit.

♦ Discharges permitted under the Protocol of 1978 relating to the International Convention for the Prevention of Pollution from Ships, 1973.

♦ Discharges permitted because the quantities, times, locations, circumstances, or conditions have been determined by the President, or by regulation, not to be harmful.

OPA exemptions:

♦ The discharge is permitted under a permit issued under Federal, State, or local law.

♦ The discharge is from a public vessel.

♦ The discharge is from an onshore facility subject to the Trans-Alaska Pipeline Authorization Act (TAPAA), 43 U.S.C. 1651, et seq.

Statute of Limitations on NRDAR

Under CERCLA Section 113(g)(1), a NRDAR claim must be brought within three years after completion of a remedial action (not including operation and maintenance) at sites that are on the National Priorities List (NPL), Federal facilities, or otherwise scheduled for CERCLA remedial action.

At sites that are not on the NPL, not Federal facilities, and not otherwise scheduled for CERCLA remedial action, a NRDAR claim must be brought within three years of the date of discovery of the loss (injury or service loss) and its connection to the release. This date may be when the injury first is documented officially, which may be the completion of the PAS.

For tribal trustees, the deadline for filing CERCLA NRDAR claims is the later of three years from the discovery of the loss and its connection to the release, or two years after the United States gives written notice to the governing body of the tribe that it will not present a claim on behalf of the tribe, or fails to present a claim within the time limitations specified elsewhere in the statute (CERCLA 126 (d)).

Under OPA Section 1017(f) (1), NRDAR actions must be brought within three years after the date on which the loss and the connection of the loss with the discharge in question is made, or the date of completion of the NRDAR assessment.

Trustees and PRPs often interpret documentation of the discovery of an injury and its connection to the release differently. Any statute of limitations analysis should be done in consultation with the Office of the Solicitor early in the development of a NRDAR case.

3.4.6   Decision to Initiate NRDAR

If the PAS criteria are affirmative (see Section 3.4.2), and at least one known and viable PRP is connected with the release or spill, NRDAR may be warranted. In making the determination to conduct NRDAR, the Coordinator also should consider other strategic and financial factors, including the following:

♦ Is there a need to address a loss of natural resource services? Even if response actions achieve restoration goals, there may be public losses pending full restoration. An extended time period before the natural resources return (or natural recovery) to their baseline condition could call for further NRDAR to compensate the public for the interim losses of resource services.

♦ If additional data collection is necessary, are there feasible and cost-effective methods of determining and quantifying injuries? Will extensive investigation or analysis be necessary to determine and quantify injuries and damages? Will other agencies and trustees be involved in such activities?

♦ Are staff resources available in the BLM and co-trustee agencies, and is management committed to undertake the activities that will be involved in conducting the assessment?

♦ Is it likely that there are feasible and cost-effective restoration actions that address primary and compensatory restoration needs? Is the restoration need thought to be large enough to make the anticipated assessment worthwhile?

♦ What is the likelihood of receiving funding support for assessment and restoration from Federal funding sources, such as the DOI Restoration Fund (for CERCLA hazardous substance releases) or the NPFC (for oil spills), or the BLM itself?

♦ Is there sufficient time to complete an assessment and determine restoration needs and damages within the time-frame for the BLM to exert its trustee authorities under the law? Are there statute of limitations concerns (see the box in Section 3.4.5)?

The Coordinator should consult with specialists within the BLM, the involved DOI bureaus, and other co-trustee agencies to address the questions above. Based on these considerations, the Coordinator should be prepared to make a recommendation on whether to proceed with NRDAR. The formal decision by the BLM to initiate NRDAR is made by the State Director, in consultation with the Solicitor, and jointly with co-trustees. The decision to proceed with NRDAR need not be unanimous among the agencies considering it; an agency may determine that, for its resource interests, NRDAR is not warranted.

At this point, the Coordinator and co-trustees should begin to formulate a case strategy with the assistance of the Solicitor. This may include consideration to approach the PRP regarding the potential for a cooperative assessment. On the other hand, the Coordinator should try to anticipate whether the PRP eventually may be open to a settlement or the case is likely to go to litigation. If the PRP may be facing bankruptcy, many other considerations may be necessary. These legal issues may bear heavily on how the Coordinator needs to proceed regarding the design and rigor of the assessment.

Not all spills or releases are substantial enough to cause significant and measurable natural resource injures, and of those that are, some do not require restoration actions supplemental to response actions. In some cases, either the injury scoping or PAS evaluations may find that no significant injuries are likely to have occurred, response actions quickly will return the resources and services to baseline condition, or natural recovery will be sufficient. In such situations, a formal NRDAR may not be necessary.

3.4.7   PAS Determination (PASD) Report

When the PAS evaluation process results in a determination that NRDAR activities are warranted, the Coordinator should document this decision in a PASD report (for CERCLA releases) or a Notice of Intent to Conduct Restoration Planning (Notice Letter; for OPA incidents). If other agencies are involved in the case, the PAS report should be prepared jointly, including all agencies' trusteeship interests. If the PAS determination is not affirmative, then no PASD report is needed, but a brief document should be prepared that records this determination for the case file.

The PASD report should be a brief and concise document that the Coordinator and co-trustees can prepare in a short time. In addition to the determinations listed above, a PASD contains information on the site and on the discharge or release; damages potentially excluded from liability under CERCLA, the CWA, or OPA; preliminary identification of pathways; exposed areas and resources; exposure concentrations; and preliminary identification of potentially injured resources and services.

A CERCLA PASD does not need to assert all potential injuries; some resource injuries may be identified during the actual assessment. The PASD becomes part of the AR for the case and part of the Report of Assessment that is prepared at the conclusion of the assessment.

An OPA notice of intent to conduct restoration planning is similar to a PASD, presenting the facts of the incident, trustee authority, natural resources and services that have likely been injured, and potential restoration actions necessary to address the injuries. If a decision about assessment methodologies has been made, the notice also may specify procedures to evaluate the injuries and to define the appropriate type and scale of restoration. The Coordinator should make the notice available to the public, deliver it to the PRP, and place it in the AR.

The DOI AO must sign the PASD, and managers from the co-trustee bureaus and other agencies must concur with the decision.

Contents of a PASD

- Information about the site
- Resource harm potentially excluded from liability
- Confirmation of release of oil or hazardous substance
- Assertion of trusteeship for affected resources
- Confirmation that the quantity and concentration of the released substances are sufficient to have caused injury
- Preliminary identification of pathways, exposed areas, resources, and concentrations
- Preliminary identification of potentially injured resources and services
- Determination that data to pursue an assessment readily are available or likely to be obtained at reasonable cost
- Determination that the response actions will not sufficiently restore injured resources and services without further action

---

3.4.8 Notice Letter to PRPs

The trustees must notify all of the identified PRPs in writing once the trustees document their determination in the PASD that an assessment is warranted. The letter must be sent before proceeding any further with NRDAR activities. The Notice Letter states the trustees' authorities and their belief that the PRPs may have liability for damages at the site. It invites the PRPs to participate in the assessment. The PASD report should be attached to the Notice Letter to provide the PRPs with the information on which the trustees have decided to proceed.

The DOI Solicitor prepares the letter, to be sent by the AO on behalf of the BLM and other DOI trustees. The Coordinator should assist the Solicitor in drafting the Notice Letter regarding the BLM resource interests, as requested. If there are other, non-DOI trustees, then the LAT sends the letter to the PRPs, with advice of the LAT legal counsel.

Under CERCLA, this is known as the Notice of Intent to Perform an Assessment, and is a separate document from the PASD; the PASD should be an attachment to the NOI letter.

Under OPA, notification is also part of the preliminary screening document and is known as the Notice of Intent to Conduct Restoration Planning. OPA restoration planning essentially consists of the same functional NRDAR activities as the assessment phase under CERCLA.

Other key contents of a notice to perform an assessment are the trustee agencies' statements of authority to assert trusteeship or co-trusteeship for the resources identified as potentially injured. Therefore, verifying each agency's legal trusteeship is critical prior to completion of the PAS and issuance of the NOI letter. The PRP is given at least 30 calendar days (with reasonable extensions, as appropriate) to respond to the notice. If the Coordinator decides to pursue a cooperative assessment with the PRPs, the Notice of Intent to Perform an Assessment may be unnecessary, or may specify the desired cooperative approach; however, this strategy should be discussed with an attorney for compliance with NRD regulations.

3.5   THE NATURAL RESOURCE DAMAGE ASSESSMENT (NRDA)

When a decision is made to proceed with NRDAR activities, the Coordinator immediately should begin planning how the NRDA for BLM resources should be conducted. This planning should consider whether an expedited assessment may be possible, or a full NRDA may be necessary. In addition to the administrative tasks, the legal, technical, scientific and analytical process for undertaking the assessment should be laid out. This begins with the Coordinator considering which resources are thought or known to be injured, and what are the most effective and technically sound ways of assessing the injuries. Additional information may be needed before the Coordinator can completely plan the assessment. At this time the Coordinator should also begin to conceptualize restoration ideas; this will aid in formulating the assessment strategy and developing more detailed restoration actions later in the assessment. Attention should also be given to identifying PRP liability and PRP viability, if not already completed. Analysis of legal defenses to liability should also be part of the early and ongoing efforts of the trustees and the Office of the Solicitor.

At this decision point, the Coordinator and other trustee representatives should jointly formulate a case strategy with the assistance of the Solicitor. As the long-term plan for the case, the case strategy should address the following:

- Technical approach to the assessment that addresses all trustee resources of concern;
- Administrative approach to coordination and public involvement; and
- Legal approach to the PRP.

The case strategy should include consideration to invite the PRP to participate in a cooperative agreement and perhaps fund the assessment. The Coordinator and other trustees on the case team should discuss strategies for reaching eventual claim resolution, which could include negotiated settlement or litigation, with the Office of the Solicitor. PRP financial viability should also be evaluated as part of strategic planning for claim resolution. This and other legal issues may be important considerations that the Coordinator and case team should factor into study designs, data quality objectives, and the overall case strategy. For example, the timing of potential settlement negotiations could be a factor in planning the extent of the assessment.

3.5.1   Introduction: Goals of the Assessment

The ultimate goal of the NRDA is to identify the actions necessary to restore injured natural resources and compensate for lost interim services. The NRDA is a planned process whereby trustees collect sound information about the injured resources and assemble the information to show that restoration actions are needed and ensure that the selected restoration actions sufficiently compensate the public. The process includes several stages: injury determination, injury quantification, and damages determination.

With the goal of restoration in mind, the Coordinator should develop and evaluate the feasibility of restoration alternatives as the assessment is implemented. If restoration planning begins during injury scoping, it should be continued throughout the assessment. Otherwise, the Coordinator should commence restoration planning when the determination is made that the NRDAR is warranted. The Coordinator may pose these questions: if a resource is injured, can it be restored and what can be done to restore it? Formulating basic restoration goals during the PAS evaluation can greatly inform the assessment planning process. The Coordinator then prepares a PED, which can be a quick and abbreviated document that used the preliminary restoration planning to help identify whether the case is worth pursuing in terms of costs and expected restoration benefits. The PED helps inform the assessment planning process.

The Coordinator should prepare an Assessment Plan describing the selected technical approach, and provide the public and PRPs an opportunity to comment. The studies conducted within this process may be done in an iterative manner, if resource conditions require, and work plans can be issued subsequent to the initial Assessment Plan. Rather than further refining the PED with additional information from any studies, the Coordinator would start development of the Preliminary Estimate of Damages and the Restoration and Compensation Determination Plan (RCDP; see Section 3.5.3.7), which specifies the procedures that the trustees will follow to estimate restoration costs and calculate the damages claim. Once the assessment information is assembled and specific restoration needs and projects become known, the trustees develop a restoration plan (see Section 3.6). A revised restoration plan is prepared once the damages claim is received.

3.5.2 The Preliminary Estimate of Damages (PED)

3.5.2.1 The PED Process

The primary purpose of the PED is to serve as a reference in scoping the Assessment Plan and NRDA process. It is an internal trustee process to ensure that the scientific, cost estimating, and valuation methodologies to be used in the damage assessment fulfill the requirements of reasonable cost. Based on readily available information, the PED helps determine if the case should go forward from a benefit-cost perspective. A PED should be used to characterize the current state of case knowledge regarding the potential damages, including data strengths and gaps; and to assist in planning or adjusting the overall assessment strategy. The PED enables the Coordinator to plan reasonable and cost-effective studies and analyses that are appropriate for the suspected injuries and service losses. Because the PED is preliminary, it is likely to be based on incomplete information about some or all of the injuries or losses. The PED may also provide a crude estimate of the case damages. Ideally, the Coordinator should conduct the PED before the Assessment Plan is drafted. However, if available data are insufficient, the PED may be completed after assessment planning, but the Coordinator should complete it as early in the assessment as possible.

The PED uses available information with applicable economic analysis. The Coordinator, with the assistance of economics expertise (see Section 2.4), estimates the anticipated costs of resource restoration of the injured resources, along with the costs of compensation for the lost services, and compares them to the anticipated costs of assessment. If the anticipated costs of the assessment are likely to exceed total damages, then the assessment strategy should be revised, or the decision to conduct NRDAR should be revisited by the co-trustees. This decision point will help focus assessment and restoration planning activities on actions that efficiently restore resources and services.

The PED is an opportunity to consider alternative ways of evaluating resource injury and service loss, categorizing potential damages, and identifying restoration options. If the information in the evaluation is sufficient, the Coordinator may also use the PED for informing preliminary settlement discussions between trustees and PRPs.

Objectives of a PED can include:

- Identification of potential reductions in natural resources and their services from injuries, which may include human-use and non-use services, as well as loss of ecological services.
- Estimation of the range of likely damages to allow for early settlement discussions about realistic restoration opportunities or the terms that would allow cash-out by the PRPs.
- Identification of injury categories that are likely to be the most important in an assessment, where "important" means the categories that are likely to be associated with the most successful restoration actions, and the categories for which injuries and damages are most reliably and accurately estimated.
- Determination of reasonable assessment costs.
- Conceptualization of potential restoration actions and the types of restoration actions that would be suitable.
- Initiation of restoration planning to provide realistic objectives for early settlement discussions.

Contents of a PED

- Description of the site
- Description of ongoing or planned response activities and their anticipated effectiveness
- Approach taken to estimate the type and amount of past and future environmental harm (injuries or service losses)
- Approach used to estimate costs or value to restore natural resources to baseline condition
- Approach used to estimate damages due to interim losses
- Total preliminary damage estimate
- Conclusions on reasonableness of pursuing NRDAR

Because it is preliminary and usually based solely on existing data, the approaches, methods, and assumptions used to develop a PED do not need to be the same approaches that the trustees ultimately choose to use for the damage determination part of the assessment. The PED should not be considered as the basis for a specific monetary claim in litigation, nor be construed to provide a definitive quantitative basis for damages. If, however, the PED is prepared when substantial injury or damages data are available, it can result in more definitive estimates of the ultimate case damages.

3.5.2.2 The PED Document

The PED process may result in an internal document for the trustees. The Coordinator need not release it to the public until the conclusion of the assessment in the Report of Assessment, but may provide it at their discretion. If it is useful for focusing the assessment and refining the damages case, the PED can be revised during the assessment as new information becomes available. The PED should be included in the Report of Assessment.

3.5.3　The Assessment Plan (AP)

3.5.3.1 Introduction

The AP presents the trustees' plan to establish that public natural resources are injured or lost and need restoration. The purpose of planning the NRDA is to ensure that the trustees conduct the assessment in a planned and systematic manner. The planning process stimulates the Coordinator to select assessment methodologies that can be conducted at reasonable cost, and potentially provides a basis to obtain funding from a cooperative PRP. In addition, the AP provides opportunities for public and PRP input. The AP informs the public and the PRPs of the investigative process of studies and analyses the trustees expect to perform to assess resource injuries and to quantify resource damages.

The CERCLA regulations direct the Coordinator to prepare an AP as part of the NRDA process, which is to be released for public review and comment. This step involves extensive internal review and co-trustee discernment because the AP is the first formal opportunity for public involvement on trustee activities. The OPA regulations do not specify the need for a formal AP as a part of the Restoration Planning Phase. The Coordinator is nevertheless encouraged to plan and document the planned assessment process for spills to provide a documented structure for the work and communicate the assessment approach to the public and the PRP for their review and comment.

3.5.3.2 Planning the Assessment

The first step in developing an AP is to select the type of procedures the Coordinator will use. For CERCLA releases, the Coordinator may select between "Type A" and "Type B" assessment procedures.

Type A procedures primarily use existing models that require minimal field observation; these models are only applicable to marine and expansive aquatic environments (see 43 CFR §11.34(a)) and are rarely used by the BLM. Type B procedures are developed specifically for individual cases and should use CERCLA regulations as guidance. If Type B procedures are followed, the assessment must confirm that at least one of the potentially injured natural resources has been exposed to the released substance.

NRDAR activities regarding OPA oil spills in coastal areas, such as the California Coastal National Monument, also tend to use assessment methods akin to the Type B procedures. Subsequent discussion in this Handbook focuses on the Type B procedures, as they are the procedures that the BLM uses most often.

Assessment Plans	
Type A Model-based for marine and expansive environments Rarely used by BLM	**Type B** Developed for individual cases and follow CERCLA guidance Used by BLM

The AP should identify methodologies for data collection and analysis for assessing specific injuries and service losses at a level of detail that is sufficient to allow determination of whether the methods proposed can be conducted at reasonable cost. "Reasonable cost" means that the costs of the injury studies, damage determination, and restoration identification are proportional to the value or importance of the resources, or not more costly than the amount of damages the trustees expect to claim.

In planning the assessment, resource specialists should review all relevant existing data and information, including information in the peer-reviewed scientific literature and government documents. This information should be used to develop hypotheses about hazardous substance transport, exposure pathways, modes of action of potentially toxic hazardous substances or oil, and the resulting significant losses of resource condition that can be addressed through restoration. With these hypotheses in mind, the Coordinator can begin to develop sampling strategies and study designs for the resources in question. Studies and analyses should have sufficient data quality to support or refute the assessment hypotheses and be defensible for use in supporting the damages claim. If necessary, the Coordinator should consult outside experts for assistance.

Oiled beach on the Oregon Coast, M/V New Carissa grounding, February 1999

The Coordinator may choose to prepare a general AP that describes the entire technical approach. As data and study needs become better defined, the Coordinator can supplement the AP with detailed sampling and analysis plans. For example, the injury determination or quantification studies may be iterative (i.e., an initial study or analysis is needed to inform the next step) to maximize efficiency and assessment success. In such cases, the Coordinator may issue subsequent study work plans and implement them, as long as they are consistent with the initial plan. Another option is to issue a complete AP in phases. As an example, for complex cases, it may be prudent to prepare and issue a plan to determine and quantify injury first, and subsequently issue the second phase of the plan for determining damages.

3.5.3.3 Assessment Strategy, Data Acquisition and Use

The AP constitutes the technical strategy and investigative process for building the damages case. The assessment should involve studies and analyses that yield data of sufficient quality to provide the level of evidence needed to prove the damages case. The Coordinator should plan the assessment in coordination with the Office of the Solicitor to ensure that elements of proof of release, pathway, exposure, injury, causation, service loss, and damages can be demonstrated clearly and logically by the data collected. Part of the technical case strategy is to determine which resources to assess and how to do so most cost-effectively. Trustees typically rely on a combination of existing data and targeted assessment studies to determine and quantify resource injuries and damages. The AP should define the intended approach for compiling and reviewing historical and current information regarding baseline and affected area conditions. The results of any ongoing monitoring programs also should be examined. The AP should specify that the trustees will evaluate the quality and reliability of any existing data and use only reliable and relevant data.

Existing information is supplemented by targeted site-specific studies, where necessary, to determine and quantify injury and damages. Where injuries to multiple resources may exist, studies can be targeted to assess "indicator" resource injuries or supporting habitats. An AP that considers indicator resources and services maximizes the efficiency of the assessment and avoids the potential for double counting.

Even while the AP is being implemented, the Coordinator and case team—including the Office of the Solicitor— should routinely evaluate the legal and technical strategy to ensure that the assessment is yielding information and data to develop a reasonable and defensible damages claim. The assessment should produce data that can be used to evaluate connections between the release and the injury or service loss, and the degree, spatial, and temporal extent of the injury or service loss. The Coordinator should maintain a record of the assessment by resource and service and update it regularly with evaluations of data certainty and strength of evidence. This record could be used to manage the assessment, evaluate and update the technical strategy, formulate the damages claim, and prepare the Report of Assessment. This document, along with the PED, preliminary data evaluations, and similar documents, are internal trustee documents that are extremely confidential. The BLM and other trustees should protect these data and information under a trustee confidentiality agreement.

3.5.3.4 The Assessment Plan Document

The AP is a publicly reviewed document that describes the studies and analyses to be performed. It must be signed by the AO, with the concurrence of the equivalent managers of the co-trustee agencies. An AP describes the procedures that will be used to assess injuries and quantify the damages. The purpose of the AP is to ensure that the assessment is conducted in a well-planned manner and at a reasonable cost. A draft AP must be made available for PRP and public review and comment for at least 30 days.

Contents of an AP

- Geographic scope of the assessment area
- Relevant site history and operations
- Description of the natural resources and the services they provide
- Assertion of trusteeship or co-trusteeship for resources
- A confirmation of hazardous substances releases and exposure of natural resources
- Sampling and analysis plans: locations, numbers, and types of samples, and analyses to be performed
- Plans for identification, review, and analysis of existing data
- Plans for quantification of resource or service losses, and costs or values of restoration
- A preliminary determination of the resource recovery period
- Demonstration that studies have been coordinated with response actions performed pursuant to the NCP
- Procedures for sharing data, split samples, or analytical results with co-trustees and the PRP
- A Quality Assurance Project Plan (QAPP) with data quality objectives for sampling and analysis

3.5.3.5 Public Review of the Assessment Plan

For CERCLA cases, the AP must be provided to the public and the PRP for review and comment. Each part of a phased AP, including the RCDP, has the same provisions for public comment and response. The comment period is 30 days, with reasonable extensions granted. Comments received must be addressed, but the Coordinator needs to prepare a revised plan for PRP and public review only if significant changes to the draft plan are deemed necessary. Comments, and the manner in which they are addressed, are included in the Report of Assessment. Detailed study plans prepared subsequent to and consistent with the AP can be made available in the Administrative Record. The detailed study plans do not need to be issued for public review and comment.

3.5.3.6 Plan Modifications

Modifications to the AP may be made as the assessment is implemented, if analyses indicate that changes in the technical strategy are necessary. Substantial changes in the assessment strategy could require that the Coordinator prepare an assessment plan amendment for public and PRP review and comment. The Coordinator should review the AP regularly throughout the assessment to ensure that the plan remains relevant and cost-effective. The Coordinator should also consult with the Solicitor to ensure that the important legal issues continue to be addressed if the assessment plan is modified.

3.5.3.7 The Restoration and Compensation Determination Plan (RCDP)

The RCDP identifies a reasonable number of possible restoration alternatives and selects the preferred alternative or alternatives. It provides an explanation of the appropriateness of the selected alternative together with an explanation of the methodologies that will be used to determine the costs of the selected alternative or alternatives. The compensable value of any public losses should also be part of the evaluation process of any restoration alternatives under the RCDP. The RCDP is an integral part of the assessment process insofar as it discloses how the assessment information will be used to arrive at the damages claim. The RCDP is a process step under CERCLA; CERCLA regulations (43 CFR §11.81) instruct trustees to conduct the RCDP process and prepare a RCDP document as part of assessment planning. Under OPA regulations, the RCDP is not a separately identified process or document, but the same objectives as the RCDP are achieved in the course of restoration planning. Under both regulations, the Coordinator may use other existing plans in the consideration and development of restoration options, if they contain restoration actions that are consistent with the restoration goals of the case.

> For all assessment studies proposed, the Coordinator, in consultation with co-trustees and any cooperative PRPs, should consider the resources available (funding, expertise, equipment, and time) and ensure cost-effectiveness and cost reasonableness of the studies and analyses undertaken.

The purposes of the RCDP are to organize how the costs will be determined and to disclose this information to the public. Planning and describing this determination process may be important for ensuring a thorough process and accurate results. Case damages include all restoration and compensation costs, including the labor of the BLM staff involved in conducting or overseeing the actions, the costs of pilot projects, analyses, environmental reviews, and other predictable costs. The more complicated the resource injuries and/or service losses are, the greater the need to plan how the Coordinator will determine the damages. Note that BLM assessment costs using BLM appropriations also are part of the ultimate damages claim.

The Coordinator should plan how the restoration and compensation damages will be determined when it becomes possible to identify the necessary restoration actions. The RCDP sets out alternatives for restoring injured natural resources and lost services and identifies the preferred alternative. The RCDP describes the methodologies the trustees will use to determine restoration and compensation costs of the preferred alternative.

The RCDP should be part of the AP if the Coordinator has enough information at that time about injuries and possible restoration goals to describe the process to determine the restoration and compensation costs. Often, however, sufficient information is not available at the time of AP development, so the regulations allow for the RCDP to be done later during injury determination or quantification. The trustees may prepare the RCDP after the Coordinator quantifies the injuries and appropriate restoration alternatives, and can identify a preferred alternative set of actions.

The Coordinator should conduct the following activities during the RCDP process:

♦ List a reasonable number of alternatives for restoration, rehabilitation, replacement, or acquisition of equivalent resources and the related services lost to the public associated with each alternative;

♦ Identify the preferred alternative, including all of the actions needed to achieve sufficient primary restoration and compensation for service losses;

♦ Provide the rationale for selecting the preferred alternative; and

♦ Identify methods to be used to determine the cost of the selected alternative and the compensable value of services lost to the public (see 43 CFR §11.83).

If the RCDP is not included in the AP, the Coordinator may elect to prepare a separate RCDP document for public review and comment. Alternatively, the Coordinator may release the RCDP within the Report of Assessment at the conclusion of the assessment. If the RCDP is part of the Report of Assessment, it should describe the determination process. The Report of Assessment describes the results of the RCDP (See *Report of Assessment*, following).

3.5.4 The Assessment: Injury Determination and Quantification

3.5.4.1 Introduction

The Coordinator and other trustee representatives should follow the AP in implementing the NRDA. Assessments can be complicated and lengthy, depending on the technical complexity of the site, the number of suspected injuries and service losses, the number and types of studies or analyses required, and timeframes for coordinating among trustee agencies and response agencies. For example, each injured resource or service loss may require its own iterative line of studies and analyses, and changes in technical direction or strategy could become necessary, based on incoming trustee information or response activities. Coordinators should remain vigilant throughout the assessment and be prepared to adjust assessment activities and modify the AP, if necessary, in response to newly acquired information that affects the assessment conduct or strategy.

In most cases, the injury scoping or PAS process may be established if hazardous substances or oil contamination has been identified as potentially or actually impacting trust resources. Based on this information, the "injury determination" phase of the assessment includes the following steps:

♦ **Injury determination** – Determines adverse effects that meet definitions of injury at 43 CFR §11.62 or 15 CFR §990.30, or other relevant injury categories. It may be possible to demonstrate injury in a laboratory, using accepted and applicable literature information.

♦ **Pathway determination** – Identifies pathways of exposure of injured natural resources to hazardous substances or oil.

Quantify injuries to natural resources to provide information for determining damages. Quantification includes several key components:

♦ **Characterization of baseline condition:** quantification of the condition of the resources and their services that would exist if the release or spill causing the injury had not happened.

♦ **Quantification of spatial and temporal extents of injury:** determination of the spatial and temporal extents of injuries, compared with baseline condition and level of service, using contaminant data, biological response data, historical records, and human-use information.

♦ **Quantification of spatial and temporal extents of service losses:** determination of the services that normally are provided by the natural resources under baseline condition and comparison to services provided in the assessment area following the release.

♦ **Quantification of recovery to baseline:** estimation of the time needed for injured resources and the services they provide to recover to baseline levels of service, usually including several realistic response and baseline (primary) restoration scenarios.

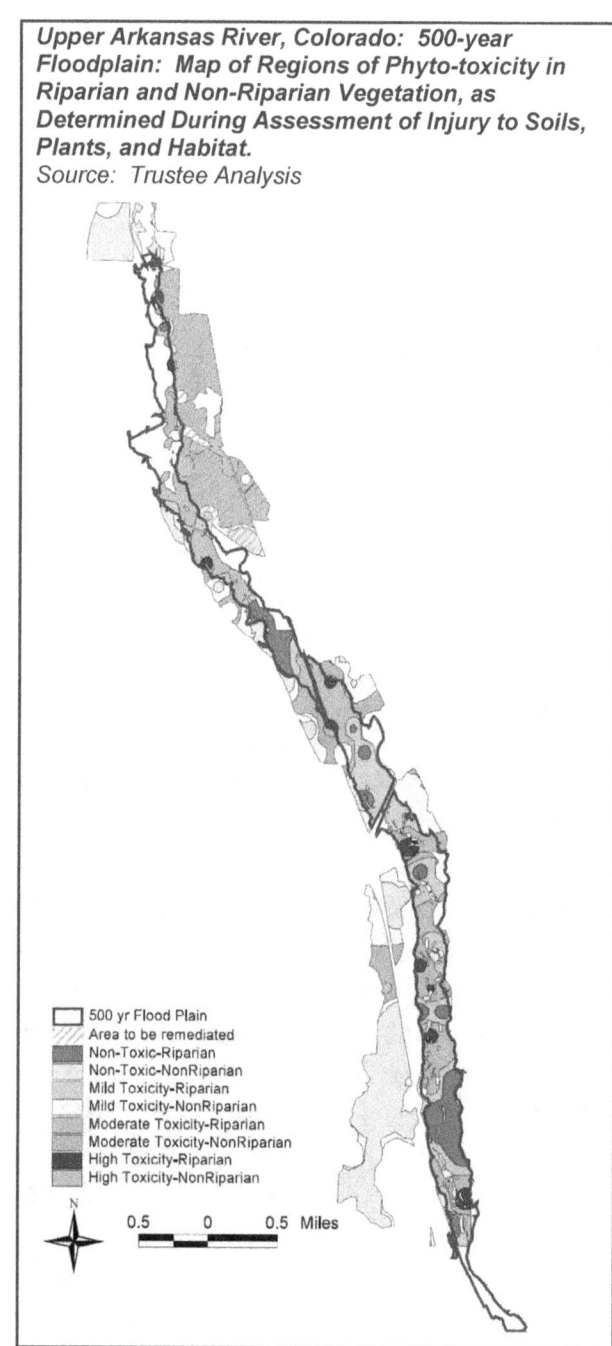

Upper Arkansas River, Colorado: 500-year Floodplain: Map of Regions of Phyto-toxicity in Riparian and Non-Riparian Vegetation, as Determined During Assessment of Injury to Soils, Plants, and Habitat.
Source: Trustee Analysis

3.5.4.2 Injury Determination

The trust resources of concern to the BLM are the resources on or affecting the BLM-managed public land: surface water, sediments, soils, vegetation, fish and wildlife, habitat functions, and other resource services.

Injury determination is the measurable observation that a resource is injured. The CERCLA regulations include definitions of injury for five resource categories. The Coordinator only needs to confirm that a single definition of injury is satisfied to "determine" injury for a given resource. Sometimes it may be technically prudent and scientifically possible to demonstrate that more than one injury definition is met for that resource. For injury definitions that involve comparisons to applicable standards—such as ground water and surface water criteria—trustees should use the most stringent, applicable standard or criterion, if several applicable standards or criteria are available. If a comparison to criteria and thresholds is insufficient to determine injury, testing methods exist to confirm injury in laboratory and field settings. Both laboratory and field testing may be necessary to demonstrate that the injury response is seen under controlled and field conditions.

Trustees can consider injuries not explicitly identified or defined in CERCLA or OPA regulations, as the regulations do not prohibit the use of other injury definitions (e.g., 43 CFR §11.10). For example, a demonstration of loss of the services can be defined as the "measurable adverse change . . . in the chemical or physical quality . . . of a natural resource" resulting from the release of hazardous substances (43 CFR §11.14 (v)). Of particular interest to the BLM could be the loss of habitat services caused by hazardous substance or oil effects on forage, shelter, security cover, or other habitat attributes. Even though there is no formally defined injury to habitat in CERCLA or OPA NRDAR regulations, a resource comprising part of the habitat, such as vegetation, can be considered injured if a service depending on that resource is lost because of the contaminant.

To determine injury, the Coordinator must determine the pathway by which the oil or hazardous substances were transported to the injured resource, in addition to meeting injury definitions. Pathway determination may rely on demonstrating the presence of the hazardous substance or oil in the pathway resource (e.g., water, sediments, soil, or plants) or by modeling. The Coordinator should consider collecting data that characterize relevant fate and transport aspects of the release or spill for pathway determination, including, for example, the spatial extent of the release or spill, and the movement, transformation, or degradation of oil or substances over time. DOI regulations note that pathway determination may be accomplished by the "demonstration of sufficient concentrations in the pathway for it to have carried the substance to the injured resources" (51 FR 27684). Pathways can be determined using a combination of information about the nature and transport mechanisms of the hazardous substances, potential pathways, and data documenting the presence of the hazardous substance in the pathway resource. Pathway determination may involve fate and transport analysis or modeling to demonstrate the sequence by which the hazardous substances or byproducts in the soil came to be located there, or came to have the characteristics of the materials discovered.

For all sampling where statistical inference is part of estimating the spatial or temporal extent or degree of injury, the sampling design should include sufficient replication and distribution to allow for rigorous analysis and extrapolation.

3.5.4.3 Baseline Condition

It is essential that the Coordinator characterize the baseline resource condition (i.e., its condition absent the release or spill in question) to determine the difference between the pre-release and the post-release resource condition or level of service. This difference will determine the extent of injury and magnitude of restoration or service replacement required. Baseline can be determined from related reference areas or pre-release resource descriptions. Baseline condition determination is a strategic and technical element of the assessment that often combines natural sciences and economics, as well as public policy and legal considerations.

> **Baseline Conditions**
>
> Site-specific conditions that would exist except for the specific release or spill in question. This may or may not be "pristine" conditions.

The DOI NRDAR regulations recommend using historical data

about a site to characterize baseline condition, if such data are available. However, if sufficient quantitative historical data are not available, the regulations suggest using data from control areas that are as close and similar to the site as possible. In experimental design, a "control" is identical to the test subject, except for the effect under assessment. Because field factors cannot be controlled easily, it may be best to use a "reference area"—an area that is similar to the assessment area in most factors that could affect the endpoint being measured—except for exposure to the release. In practice, several reference areas are often identified to characterize a normal range of baseline conditions.

It is imperative to give careful consideration to all of the factors contributing to the "condition but for the release in question" that affect the baseline condition. There may be intense scrutiny of the methods and approaches used to define baseline. Baseline services can be affected by conditions and activities that are not related to the release. Natural and anthropogenic factors such as natural mineralization, naturally erosive soils, roads, construction, permitted land uses, and other agricultural practices can adversely affect soil and water quality and the biota supported by natural resources. Therefore, reference areas should be selected to match assessment sites in terms of relevant physical, chemical, biological, and socio-economic conditions.

Factors unrelated to the release that affect baseline condition should be carefully analyzed in terms of their influence on the degree of injury. For example, although wildlife naturally experiences stress related to climate or food availability and quality, added stress imposed by the release of hazardous substances could exceed a stress tolerance threshold, causing injuries to wildlife. In such a case, injury is caused by the additional stressor (the release) and not by the natural (non-chemical) stressors in the environment.

At sites where more than one PRP has released hazardous substances that have caused injury, the trustees may not need to apportion the damages liability among the PRPs, although they may need to characterize baseline conditions regarding specific injuries and service losses. If, however, NRDAR is being conducted to assess the effects of only certain hazardous substances and other substances (hazardous or non-hazardous) are present in the environment but not attributable to the PRP in question, then those substances may have to be considered as part of the baseline condition.

3.5.4.4 Quantification of Resource Injury

Injury quantification is the counting of the amount, degree, extent, and duration of the resource injury. The Coordinator should quantify the effects of the release or spill for use in identifying the actions needed to restore the injured resources. Quantification of injury includes the following:

- **Quantification of spatial and temporal extents of injury:** determination of the spatial and temporal extents of injuries using contaminant data, biological response data, historical records, and human-use information.

- **Quantification of injury compared to baseline:** determination of the amount or quality of the resource under baseline condition and comparison to the resource condition of the assessment area following the release.

- **Quantification of recovery to baseline:** quantification of the time needed for injured resources to recover to baseline levels, based on realistic response and primary restoration scenarios, and natural recovery without restoration.

The Coordinator should determine the difference between the baseline condition and the injured condition. The baseline condition is characterized at reference locations or in pre-release resource descriptions. The Coordinator may need to conduct field sampling or laboratory tests to address specific hypotheses about sources, transport pathways, potentially exposed biological or other resources, and system dynamics that could affect the degree or extent of injury or service loss. The Coordinator should consider collecting data that characterize relevant fate and transport aspects of the release for pathway determination, including, for example, the spatial extent of the release, and the movement, transformation, or degradation of substances over time. In addition, economic techniques can determine the quantity of injury or service loss. Many of these data may be available from the response investigations conducted at the site but the Coordinator may need to look beyond the response investigation area to quantify all significant injuries. Determinations of injury to fish, wildlife, and birds should consider the extent of impact (i.e. whether individuals, local populations, or more widespread populations are affected by the release or spill).

Approaches to estimating the extent and degree of injury may include the use of chemical, toxicological, biological, or economic data, Geographic Information System (GIS) analyses, or modeling. If the degree and duration of injury and services varies spatially, the injured areas can be divided into sections for quantification of injuries and services.

The Coordinator should consider the interaction of resource injuries and service losses. As an example, high toxic metals contents in riparian zone soils, causing barren areas surrounded by diverse vegetation, would confirm injury to the affected soils, and also to the plant community that should be present at that site. On such sites, the vegetation is unable to survive because of phyto-toxicity of the injured soils. The absence of the expected vegetation at that site also means that the site has lost the services the vegetation would provide as habitat to birds and wildlife, as well as bank stabilization against erosion by the nearby river.

Fishing health warning along barren sections of stream habitat downstream of historic copper mining complex

3.5.4.5 Quantification of Service Loss

Quantification of service loss is the counting of the amount, degree, extent, and duration of the loss of a service provided by a resource. The Coordinator should quantify the effects of the release or spill for use in identifying the actions needed to compensate for the lost services. Quantification of service loss includes the following:

♦ **Quantification of spatial and temporal extents of service loss:** determination of the spatial and temporal extents of service losses using contaminant data, biological response data, historical records, and human-use information.

♦ **Quantification of service losses compared to baseline:** determination of the services that are normally provided by the natural resources under baseline condition and comparison to services provided in the assessment area following the release.

♦ **Quantification of recovery to baseline:** quantification of the time needed for recovery of lost resource services to baseline levels, based on realistic response and primary restoration scenarios, and natural recovery without restoration.

The Coordinator should determine the difference between the level of resource services provided in the injured condition and the level of resource services provided in the baseline condition. This differential should be determined over the entire duration of the injured condition. The differential may change over the course of that time period. Table 3-1 identifies natural resource services that could be reduced as a result of contamination of resources and pathways. Loss of, or reduction in, natural resource services is the basis for determining the extent of service replacement needed. The injury definitions identified in CERCLA and OPA guidance do not address service loss directly. However, quantification of injury, service loss, and damages is necessary in addition to determination of injury.

Service losses associated with surface water injuries include the following:

♦ Drinking water supply disruption at a recreational use area;

♦ Recreational use (e.g., swimming, boating, or fishing) closures for some duration of time;

♦ Adverse effects on aquatic biota or aquatic habitat;

♦ Accumulation of substances in the aquatic food chain leading to adverse effects on biota;

♦ Reduced assimilative capacity of a wetland or body of water; and

♦ Reduced ability of wetland or body of water to absorb low levels of contaminants without exceeding standards or without adverse effects (51 Fed. Reg. 27716, August 1, 1986).

Service losses associated with ground water injuries include the following:

♦ Drinking water supply disruption at a recreational use area;

♦ Preclusion of future use of an aquifer as a public drinking water supply at an existing or planned recreational use area;

♦ Closure of a recreational use area because of the risk associated with a ground water plume; and

♦ Habitat (such as in a wetland or cavern) degradation related to the toxicity of substances in shallow ground water.

The following service losses associated with injuries to air can result from releases from transportation corridors or releases of substances from facilities upwind of public use areas:

♦ Closures of recreational use areas;

♦ Wildlife kills or plant die-offs associated with exposure to substances in the air; and

♦ Deposition of particulates transported in the air on soils, plants, or other biota causing injuries to geologic, biological, or combined habitat resources.

Service losses associated with injuries to soils include the following:

♦ Elimination or reduction of the soil's ability to provide habitat for wildlife or grazing for livestock; and

♦ Alteration or simplification of the plant community structure that diminishes wildlife habitat quality or rangeland quality.

Human use service losses associated with resource injuries include the following:

♦ Reduced access to recreational areas;

♦ Reduced quality of experience at a recreational area; and

♦ Reduced access to grazing or to the exploration or production of energy resources.

In cases where there is a measurable resource injury, there could also be a measurable service loss that accrues because of public perception about the injury. If the public is unwilling to use services arising from the injured resource because people perceive the services to be unusable or unavailable, then this could be a measurable service loss.

The CERCLA NRDAR regulations specify that injury determination and quantification may be conducted resource-by-resource. However, natural resources and the ecological services they provide are interdependent. An example of this interdependence is the habitat services for aquatic wildlife that surface water, sediments, soils, and vegetation along a stream provide, and also connectivity with other habitats for semi-aquatic and upland wildlife communities that may be dependent on access to the stream. Therefore, injuries to individual natural resources may cause ecosystem-level service reductions. The BLM should consider these interdependent ecosystem-level service losses when assessing service losses.

Table 3.1: Resources, Potential Restoration Targets, Potential Baseline or Affected Services

Potentially Injured Resource	Pathways/ Restoration Targets	Examples of Service Losses [a]
Ground water	Ground water Surface water Soils	Drinking, ecological services, and assimilative capacity[b]
Surface water	Surface water Sediments Ground water Riparian soils	Drinking, recreation, ecological services (e.g., habitat, shelter, forage), and assimilative capacity
Sediments	Surface water Sediments Ground water Riparian soils	Ecological services (e.g., habitat, shelter, forage), and assimilative capacity
Soil/geologic resources	Ground water Surface water Sediments Air	Ecological services (e.g., habitat, shelter, growth medium), access to mineral estate, and assimilative capacity
Aquatic biota	Benthic invertebrates Fish Surface water Sediments Ground water Riparian soils	Ecological services (e.g., prey for other organisms), recreational fishing, and consumption
Terrestrial resources	Soils Vegetation Surface water Sediments Ground water Terrestrial biota	Recreation (e.g., wildlife viewing), grazing, and ecological services (e.g., habitat, shelter, forage)

a. There may be damages associated with other categories not listed.
b. The ability of a resource to "absorb low levels of (contaminants) without exceeding standards or without adverse effects" (51 Fed. Reg. 27716, August 1, 1986).

3.5.4.6 Resource recoverability analysis

The Coordinator should perform a resource recoverability analysis for each injured resource during the injury quantification phase. The purpose of this analysis is to estimate how fully and quickly the injured natural resources could recover to baseline conditions. The analysis should first consider natural recovery (i.e. resource recoverability if no actions were taken); this may reveal whether the injured resource would recover enough on its own so that response and restoration actions are not needed.

The Coordinator should conduct resource recoverability analysis if planned or implemented response actions are taken. If response actions are taken but injured conditions remain, the resource recoverability analysis should estimate the residual recovery time for possible alternatives for restoration, rehabilitation, replacement, or acquisition of equivalent resources. Usually, the less extensive the response action is, the more extensive the restoration action would need to be. The more extensive the restoration is, in bringing the resource back to baseline more quickly, the less interim service loss may exist requiring compensation. This analysis might involve the following:

◆ Comparison to similar events or cleanups elsewhere;

◆ Consideration of ecological succession and the time required for ecosystem recovery following the disturbance;

◆ Biological generation times; or

◆ Running chemical or hydrological models to estimate the time required to reach baseline chemical conditions under alternative scenarios.

A Brief Example of the Meaning of and Relationship between Injuries, Service Losses, Damages, and Primary and Compensatory Restoration

Injuries are specific, measurable effects on the physical, biological, or chemical quality of natural resources. The intent of NRDAR is to restore the natural resources that are injured. Restoring the injured resources is called primary or baseline restoration. Natural resources also provide services that may be impacted over time because of the injury. Replacing the services that are lost from the time of injury until the resources return to baseline is compensatory restoration. Depending on the nature of the site and the type of injury, trustees may need to consider restoration alternatives that address primary and compensatory losses. If a site has both primary and compensatory injury and loss, damages would be composed of alternatives that would compensate the public for both primary restoration and compensate for the lost resource services.

For example, primary restoration for a release into water that kills a number of fish might involve the replacement of the number of fish that were killed. Primary restoration also is likely to include the restoration of the aquatic habitat by removing the water contaminant to baseline condition.

Compensatory restoration for the fish kill addresses the services the fish provide—such as food chain services or fishing recreation—that are lost in the interim from when the number of fish are killed until the equivalent number of fish are replaced (primary restoration) to the baseline population. Thus, compensatory restoration might involve restoring habitat on-site to greater than baseline condition, so that it supports more fish than baseline population, or enhancing fish habitat nearby to support additional fish, to provide all the food chain services that are being lost. It could involve developing additional fishing recreation to make up for the opportunity that is being lost in the interim until the baseline fish population is re-established.

3.5.5   Damages Determination

3.5.5.1 Purpose

The damages determination phase is intended to "establish the amount of money to be sought (from the PRP) in compensation for injuries to natural resources resulting from a . . . release of a hazardous substance" (43 CFR §11.80(b)). Damages include both the costs to restore resources to baseline service levels and compensation for service losses. It is the BLM policy to determine damages based on the cost of the necessary restoration and compensation, rather than on the intrinsic value of the injured resource or monetary value on the services lost, when possible, consistent with underlying statutory and agency preferences for restoration. Restoration consists of the "restoration, rehabilitation, replacement, or acquisition of the equivalent of the injured natural resources and the services those resources provide" (43 CFR §11.82(a)). Thus, the Coordinator should carefully identify all of the restoration necessary to offset all public losses, together with the trustees' reasonable costs of conducting the assessment, including the trustees' future costs to plan, oversee, and monitor restoration.

3.5.5.2 Restoration Goals as Basis for Damages

In the damages determination phase, the Coordinator should base this determination on the costs of the primary and compensatory restoration actions needed to restore resources to baseline conditions. These actions should be sufficient to offset the past, current, and future losses caused by natural resource injuries at the site. Restoration actions, along with response actions, should reduce injuries and return services to baseline levels more quickly than would natural recovery alone. Part of the analysis requires an assessment of the recovery period for injured resources. Actions that provide a quicker return to baseline than natural recovery have the effect of reducing the duration and amount of services lost, and hence the compensatory component of the natural resource damages.

Figure 3.1: Graph of Resource Percent Injured and Restored by Removal and Restoration Actions

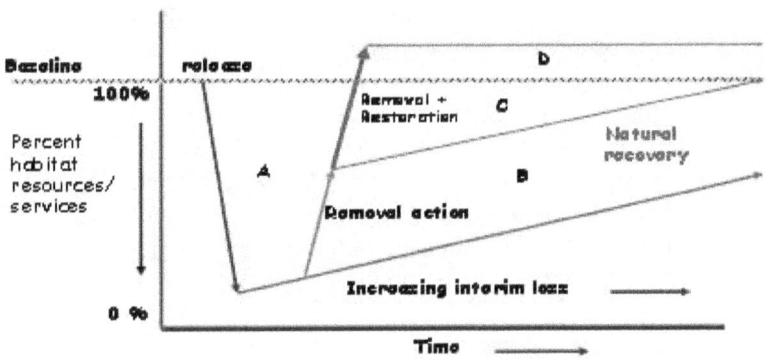

Figure 3.1 depicts how natural resource injuries and service losses accumulate over time for a hypothetical injury scenario, and how removal and remedial actions might affect the levels of habitat resources and services provided. Losses accrue for as long as natural resources and services remain (past and future) below baseline condition. The total potential resource and service loss is the area between the baseline line and the lowest sloping line trending upward to the right – Areas A, B, and C. Area A represents natural resource injuries and service losses that accrue before any action is taken. If no action is taken, the loss of resources will be A + B + C. If only a removal action is taken, then the loss is A + C. If restoration is also done, then the loss is only A. If restoration is also done to offset the loss of Area A, then Area D may be gained. To provide sufficient compensation for services lost over time, it may be necessary to conduct restoration off-site that improves natural resource services at that location and may replace those lost on-site. The critical aspect of additional restoration is that resource improvements accrue only in the future, and for as long as the baseline condition is exceeded.

3.5.5.3 Damages for Injured Resources – Primary Restoration

To determine the damages for injured resource restoration, the Coordinator determines the costs of the restoration needed to return resources to baseline condition. This element of restoration is sometimes called "primary restoration" or "baseline restoration." This determination is based on the itemized costs of the restoration actions identified in the preferred alternative. The itemized costs are based on planned restoration actions that are matched (i.e., scaled) to the quantities of injury of the various affected resources. Some restoration costs may actually be similar to construction costs itemized for a response action. Primary restoration can take place on- or off-site. The BLM prefers to restore in-kind resources on-site (i.e., resources identical to those injured), but may find it necessary to restore out-of-kind resources (i.e., resources merely similar to, or acceptable replacements for, the injured resources), if on-site restoration is not cost-effective. Also, it might be necessary to conduct this restoration off-site.

The previous NRDA steps should provide the Coordinator with sufficient information to understand the potential restoration options and determine the damages for primary restoration, particularly if restoration goals have been formulated and refined as the injury and service loss data were collected. The Coordinator may use a variety of techniques for estimating restoration costs, separately or in combination, that focus directly on the value of lost natural resources, or the cost of the required restoration, or both. Available techniques include unit cost, comparison cost, standard time data cost, construction cost, and other estimating methodologies that are dependable and commonly accepted practices. Restoration costs should include all direct and indirect costs of the actions, the labor of the BLM staff involved in the conduct or oversight of the actions, as well as the costs of the required studies or pilot projects, analyses, environmental reviews, and other predictable costs.

3.5.5.4 Damages for Interim Lost Services – Compensatory Restoration

To ascertain the compensation damages for lost services, according to CERCLA regulations, the Coordinator should determine the value of the services that have been lost in the interim. This element of restoration is sometimes called the "compensatory restoration" or "compensable value." Compensatory restoration costs relate to the value of lost ecological services and lost public uses the injured resources would provide. Public uses may even include the lost non-use values (i.e., existence values) if they can be measured.

An alternative to determining interim loss damages based on the service value is to determine the damages based on the cost of restoration actions that replace additional resource services that are equivalent to the amount of those lost over time. This restoration-based approach is consistent with OPA regulations and in practice, has been used extensively at CERCLA sites, particularly for settlement purposes. A restoration-based process can assist in achieving restoration objectives more quickly and can be a preferred basis for negotiating settlements with PRPs.

 Compensatory restoration can take place on- or off-site. The BLM prefers to restore in-kind service losses on-site (i.e., services identical to those lost), but it may be necessary to replace out-of-kind services (i.e., similar services that are acceptable replacement for the lost services). Also, it might be necessary to replace these services off-site if on-site replacement is impractical.

Interim damages are those that accrue from when the release first causes the service loss until the service returns to baseline, or some subpart of that period. Interim damages include past damages from the earliest point that injuries and losses from releases are known, or from the time of promulgation of the statute (e.g., December 1980 for CERCLA), when the BLM trustee authority began,[8] up to the present time of the assessment. Interim damages also include future damages (i.e., from the time of the assessment until restoration actions are completed) and residual damages (i.e., ongoing damages that accrue after restoration activities have ceased, if restoration does not fully restore natural resources services to baseline levels). The Coordinator should focus damages determination efforts on future damages, if obtaining damages for the entirety of interim losses is not likely.

Ideally, the Coordinator should determine the cost or value of the services that have been lost, and on that basis, identify the types and amounts of compensatory restoration that are necessary to offset those losses. The cost or value of the service actually lost may be quantifiable. For example, a human use of a resource, such as a recreation user day, may have a documented or measurable economic value. For some service losses, however, especially those relating to ecological services, it may be difficult to calculate the actual value of the services that have been lost. In such cases, the Coordinator should base the determination on establishing the costs or values of the actions needed to compensate for the services losses. This means identifying the costs to replace lost habitat services, such as purchasing lands or protective conservation easements. In such instances, the itemized costs of the actions, as identified in the preferred restoration alternative, relate directly to the quantities of service lost (i.e., the compensation actions are scaled to the losses).

3.5.5.4.1 Economic Methods for Compensable Damages Determination

The Coordinator may use various economic methods to estimate the cost or value of either the service losses or the actions needed for compensation. A number of economic tools are routinely used by trustees on NRDA cases (see 43 CFR §11.83), including:

- Market-based approaches, such as market demand and supply models;
- Fee losses and appraisal methods;

---

8. Trustees can claim for injuries that occurred before December 1980 if the injuries caused by the release continued after December 1980. In some cases, releases and injuries began before December 1980 and continue to the present.

- Added or averted cost models;
- Public preference techniques, such as travel cost, random utility models, and property valuation models;
- Factor income approaches;
- Benefit transfer or unit value measures;
- Conjoint analysis;
- Habitat equivalency analysis (HEA); and
- Resource equivalency analysis (REA).

The Coordinator should make decisions on the selection of economic tools on a case-by-case basis in consultation with economic and legal experts. The methods used should be appropriate, acceptable, and dependable measures of the service losses in question and should be usable at reasonable cost. HEA and REA are becoming commonplace in NRDAR; these methods may be used to value only ecological service losses. Lost recreation, concessions and other activities/fees associated with human uses of BLM lands are more appropriately measured by the other tools listed. These tools can be used separately or in combination, but the Coordinator should guard against the double counting of damages.

The Coordinator may find it preferable to address interim service losses by devising new primary restoration actions or enlarging those related actions that are being planned to address injuries. With this approach, the cost of the service loss compensation is the incremental cost of the new or added restoration.

The compensatory restoration costs should include all direct, indirect, and overhead costs of implementing the actions, labor, and benefits of the BLM staff involved in the conduct or oversight and monitoring of the actions, and the costs of required studies or pilot projects, analyses, environmental reviews, and other predictable costs.

3.5.5.4.2 Habitat and Resource Equivalency Analyses

Many BLM NRDAR cases involve the loss of habitat or other ecological services. As such, the Coordinator may wish to use the HEA and/or REA methodologies to estimate compensatory projects. The HEA method is typically used for habitat quality services, and the REA method is typically used for individual resources, such as a species of injured wildlife. These tools are accounting frameworks used to estimate the amount of services that must be gained by compensatory restoration or acquisition to offset or replace the amount of services lost because of the injury. For example, HEA and REA could be used regarding fish habitat to scale restoration that would improve fish populations, which could be measured in fish-years, but not for recreational fishing and the replacement of fishing-days. HEA and REA techniques are relatively simple in concept: add up all of the losses (debit) and determine the amount of restoration gain (credit) sufficient to offset the losses. The process of equating debit to credit to identify the proper quantity of restoration is called "scaling."

The HEA and REA methods can be useful tools because calculating the value of the injured resources or lost services themselves in some cases may be problematic. As an example, in the case of ecological service losses, the services themselves are not valued, but instead, the cost of their replacement becomes the measure of damages. Note that these methods involve economic analyses that should be performed by economists. Although simple in concept, the reliability of HEA and REA is completely dependent on the Coordinator's decision-making on the selection of model inputs. It is critical that the Coordinator accurately identify the specific service or resource attributes (i.e., metrics, to be measured and used in the models). HEA and REA are appropriate for scaling compensatory restoration for ecological service losses when: (1) a common metric can be defined for natural resource services that captures the level of services provided by injury and replacement habitats; (2) the landscape context of the injury and replacement habitats provides similar opportunity to supply the relevant ecological services; and (3) sufficient data on input parameters exist, or are cost-effective to collect. An example set of metrics would be acres of a specific type of habitat having a percent loss of a certain function for a number of years. For more information on identifying metrics, see Appendices D and E.

3.5.6 Pre-Claim Restoration Planning

During the damages determination phase, the Coordinator should plan the restoration actions, in order to calculate the costs for those restoration actions for the damages claim. The Coordinator identifies and scales the restoration actions that are needed, based on the injuries and losses that have been quantified. Restoration planning at this stage should build on the analysis from the RCDP as well as the results of final assessment activities. It is not subject to NEPA at this point in the NRDA process, but the information developed will be useful for post-claim restoration planning, which is subject to NEPA. Accordingly, the Coordinator should use criteria similar to those in NEPA analysis to develop viable alternatives and select the preferred alternative.

3.5.6.1 Pre-Claim Restoration Planning Objectives and Process

Pre-claim restoration planning has two objectives:

- To identify, screen, select, and scale restoration actions that would be appropriate to restore resources and services and compensate the public; and

- To formalize the trustees' intentions for restoration and establish a draft plan for restoration implementation after the damages are paid.

Pre-claim restoration planning is done primarily for the purpose of determining restoration costs. It also may greatly inform the trustees' efforts to plan and implement the eventual restoration actions, but more thorough restoration planning may be needed after the trustees receive the damages. In the pre-claim restoration planning process, the Coordinator should develop several restoration alternatives that cover a reasonable range of possibilities for accomplishing the restoration, and select a preferred alternative for the restoration, rehabilitation, replacement, and/or acquisition of the equivalent of the injured natural resources (43 CFR §11.82(a); 15 CFR §990.53).

At this pre-claim planning stage, the Coordinator should design alternatives that address all of the injuries and service losses in the case. In selecting alternatives, the trustees should attempt to select restoration actions that, as a package, would make the environment and public whole. The design of alternatives and selection of the preferred alternative should be deliberated by all co-trustees during the assessment process. If there is a possibility of settlement before the final damages claim is determined, the prospect of the settlement may affect the extent of the restoration alternatives being planned.

To properly evaluate the alternatives and to prepare for the environmental analysis that will be part of final restoration planning later, the Coordinator should develop and apply screening and ranking criteria that are relevant to consideration of the relative environmental impacts and benefits of the alternatives. These criteria should be the same as or similar to those used in the post-claim plan. Based on the evaluation criteria, the Coordinator should then evaluate the alternatives and select a preferred alternative. The Coordinator then describes the alternatives and preferred alternative in the RCDP. The Coordinator should ensure that the documentation supporting the preferred restoration alternative includes a reasonably detailed rationale for its selection as such, to explain and defend the selection in negotiations or court. The Coordinator should use evaluation criteria that satisfy any requirements or preferences imposed by relevant State or Federal NRDAR statutes and regulations, as well as BLM and other trustee agencies' natural resource management mandates.

With the preferred alternative selected, the Coordinator can determine the restoration costs, according to the RCDP. These costs include both primary and compensatory restoration components of the preferred alternative, and also future planning, implementation, maintenance, and monitoring costs. The processes used to develop alternatives, select the preferred alternative, and determine costs are then documented in the RCDP.

> **The Coordinator should consider the following process for determining restoration-based damages:**
>
> ◆ Establish evaluation criteria for evaluating restoration and compensation options for each injury and service loss.
>
> ◆ Develop a list or database of potential restoration and compensation options.
>
> ◆ Summarize the restoration and compensation proposals into categories of actions.
>
> ◆ Apply evaluation criteria to identify categories or potential restoration and compensation actions that meet pass-fail criteria, and then to rank the remaining categories or actions to select the preferred options.
>
> ◆ Choose appropriate metrics for comparing and scaling the preferred restoration and compensation options with the resource injuries and service losses they would address.
>
> ◆ Develop information about unit costs for the preferred restoration and compensation actions. Costs should account for the implementation and administration of the action, as well as operation, maintenance, and monitoring expenditures required to ensure that the project provides the restoration or compensation benefits necessary.

The Coordinator should try to identify the proper metrics for scaling the restoration actions and collect information on unit restoration costs at the time that the potential actions are being developed and refined. Undertaking these tasks concurrently may enable the Coordinator to determine the potential costs and benefits of the restoration actions before developing the proposed restoration alternatives or evaluating them against the screening and ranking criteria. The development of restoration options is often an iterative process that may include input from outside the trustee council. The trustees could receive restoration proposals during or after they initially categorize the potential projects into restoration alternatives.

Under OPA, the restoration plan is the document that summarizes the injury assessment information collected during the restoration planning phase and lays out the plans for restoring injured resources. The restoration plan presents the injury assessment procedures used; describes the nature, degree, and extent of injuries; presents the goals, objectives, and restoration alternatives; and selects a tentative preferred alternative. It also should include a description of the involvement of the PRP and a plan for how the Coordinator will evaluate the restoration projects for effectiveness. The Coordinator makes the draft plan available for public review and comment, after which the final plan is developed. The final plan includes responses to comments. If public comment results in substantial changes to the draft plan, a summary of the changes is included in the final plan.

The Coordinator may find it useful to consider restoration goals or actions that address existing resource management plans (RMP) or activity plans of the BLM or other agencies, academic experts, and the public. Under CERCLA, if the trustees use other existing plans, they should reference the plans regarding specific actions in the preparation of the case-specific restoration plan. Under OPA, if the trustees use other existing plans instead of preparing a case-specific plan, they should prepare a public notice of intent that describes the injuries, the restoration project, and how the project adequately compensates the environment and the public for injuries. The PRP may propose project alternatives that meet trustee objectives, particularly if a cooperative assessment is underway. The Coordinator should be continuously mindful of restoration possibilities throughout the assessment to help focus and strengthen the studies and analyses.

3.5.6.2 Locations for Restoration or Compensation Actions

The Coordinator should consider restoration actions that directly address the injuries and service losses (i.e., on-site restoration of the injured resources). Projects that are conducted on or as close as possible to the location of the injured resource are preferred. However, if there is a reasonable resource connection or if administrative factors intervene, the Coordinator could consider restoration actions at a location that is geographically removed from the site of the injury. In some cases, the exact injured resource or lost service may not be restorable, but similar resources or services elsewhere that meet overall restoration goals and are acceptable to the public could be restored or enhanced. There also may be existing management plans regarding the same resources locally or regionally that identify desired or proposed actions to improve resource conditions. An RMP, for example, may identify areas that the BLM regards as having high resource value or where the BLM would like to acquire important habitat or further develop recreation opportunity. These RMP contents could provide bases for aspects of restoration planning. A project or action identified in a resource management plan that is not already funded and that addresses resources or services injured by the release could be considered as a NRDAR restoration alternative.

3.6   POST ASSESSMENT

3.6.1   Required Documentation

The post assessment phase is the final step before the damages claim is presented for settlement or litigation. This phase follows the conclusion of the NRDA that was conducted by the Coordinator and co-trustees to identify the necessary and preferred restoration actions and their costs. This information is presented, with supporting documents, in the CERCLA Report of Assessment or the OPA Restoration Plan. The Coordinator should make the draft of either document available for public review and comment. Following the public comment period, a final Report of Assessment or restoration plan is prepared that includes responses to comments and a summary of changes made to the draft plan.

3.6.1.1 CERCLA Required Documentation

When the Coordinator completes the NRDA, a Report of Assessment is prepared. This document presents the conclusions of the assessment based on the outcome of the investigative and analytical work completed according to the AP. The Report of Assessment presents the injuries, the amount of service loss, and the restoration that is needed to restore injured resources and lost services. The Report of Assessment also collects the major documents of the NRDAR process.

The CERCLA Report of Assessment includes the following:

- All documentation supporting the injury determination and quantification, including the scientific and analytical results of methodologies used;
- All documentation supporting the damages quantification phase, including scientific and analytical results;
- The PASD and the PED;
- The AP, public comments on the AP, and trustee responses to those comments; and
- The RCDP, public comments on the RCDP, and trustee responses to those comments.

3.6.1.2 OPA Required Documentation

Under OPA regulations, when the Coordinator completes the restoration planning phase, a restoration plan document is prepared that summarizes the injury assessment and lays out the plans for restoring injured resources. A restoration plan presents the following:

- The injury assessment procedures used;
- The nature, degree, and extent of injuries;
- The goals, objectives, and restoration alternatives;
- A tentative preferred alternative;
- A description of the involvement of the PRP and the public; and
- A plan for how the restoration projects will be evaluated for effectiveness.

3.6.2   Damages Claim and Demand Letter

The Coordinator should ensure the preparation of the damages claim at the conclusion of the assessment. The claim contains the findings of the final CERCLA Report of Assessment or OPA Restoration Plan. Under both statutes, the trustees may present the damages claim to the PRP in a demand letter. The Solicitor plays the primary role in issuing the demand letter and related activities. The demand letter requests that the PRP either implement restoration or pay the trustees a specified amount of monetary damages to implement restoration. This amount includes the trustees' direct and indirect costs necessary to complete all actions identified in the selected alternative for restoration, rehabilitation, replacement, and/or acquisition of equivalent resources. The amount also includes the trustees' reasonable past costs of assessment and future costs of implementing restoration. It is important to remember that both the BLM-appropriated and DOI-allocated assessment costs are recoverable and should be included in the damages claim, based on sufficient documentation (see Section 2.5.2 through 2.5.4).

The demand letter should establish the date of the PRP receipt. It should include information about the site, the release or spill, the statutory basis for trusteeship, the injuries, the final restoration plan, an index to the AR, and the damages claim. The PRP has 60 days to respond in writing to the damages claim. If portions of the damages liabilities have been allocated among several PRPs, separate claims may be needed for each PRP. If the PRP does not respond to the demand in a timely manner, the trustees may seek authority to file suit.

The transmittal of the demand letter to the PRPs may result in settlement negotiations, agreement to seek agreeable terms that could lead to settlement or litigation. Under OPA, if the PRP does not agree to the demand in settlement, the trustees may file a claim in court within three years after the public release of the final restoration plan. For OPA cases, the trustees also may file a claim for reimbursement from the Oil Spill Liability Trust Fund if the damages are not available from the PRP. For CERCLA cases, the PRP is the only source for obtaining natural resource damages, either through settlement or litigation. Under CERCLA, there are two different periods, depending on the site response status. If the site is in the remedial process under CERCLA 104 or 106 actions, such as at EPA National Priorities List (NPL) sites, the trustees must file the claim in court within three years after the completion of the remedy. If the site is not under these response actions, the trustees must file a claim in court within three years of their discovery of the release and its connection to the injury.

Depending on which avenue the case takes, the Coordinator may need to provide substantial supporting documentation, as deemed necessary by the Solicitor and the DOJ legal representative.

3.6.3 Claim Report for Negotiations and Legal Issues

The Coordinator should complete a claim report that characterizes the elements of the claim, based on the outcome of the assessment activities, for use in preparing for negotiations or litigation. The claim report is an internal, highly confidential document that describes the details of the damages claim. The Solicitor on the trustee council should be directly involved in this preparation. The claim report has two purposes: (1) to provide managers and trustees a concise characterization of the damages claim and its elements; and (2) to enable attorneys to view all of the cost items to develop optimal strategies for negotiating the trustees' restoration and cost reimbursement priorities.

The claim report itemizes past assessment costs, including direct and indirect costs; restoration and compensation action implementation costs, operations and management, and monitoring costs; and administrative costs related to future oversight of restoration actions and monitoring. Past assessment costs include all the BLM appropriations and DOI Restoration Fund dollars that were spent on assessment activities. The claim report contains more details than are presented to the public and PRPs.

The claim report might reference potential issues that may require additional scrutiny in the future and might impede the trustees from granting a covenant not to sue. For example, if the proposed restoration actions are sufficiently untested and risky, the negotiators might require that portions of a settlement be left "open" until sufficient success or compensation has been demonstrated.

The Coordinator also should consider other details about the assessment as additional contents of the internal claim report. In settlement discussions, negotiators may make reasonable, worst-case scenario assumptions or other kinds of professional judgments in developing estimates of injury and service loss quantification and restoration scaling. This is an acceptable part of the NRDAR process. Because of this, negotiators should understand the bases for the damage claim elements—including both the types of factual information used in the assessment and the types of assumptions and professional decisions made—and how any uncertainties might affect the damages claim.

The claim report might discuss considerations about how to structure settlement agreements, such as whether to request funding for the trustees to implement restoration, to request that the PRP implement restoration, or a combination of the two. If specific projects have been identified, it might be more cost effective to have the PRP implement restoration actions. Alternatively, if the trustees' relationship with the PRP does not allow such an agreement to be reached, or if the PRP is eager to reach closure on restoration obligations, then the trustees might wish to receive cash settlement instead and implement the restoration projects themselves.

3.6.4 Damages Claim Settlement or Litigation

In most NRDAR cases, the trustees and PRPs reach a settlement. With the assistance of the Solicitor and others, the Coordinator should anticipate whether the case is likely to reach settlement or end in litigation, and proceed accordingly in developing and conducting the NRDA. In some cases litigation might be required, for example, if the PRPs contest the trustees' technical information or their liability. The Coordinator should assist the Solicitor in preparing for litigation, understanding that extensive documentation and other technical efforts are part of that process.

In the event of a settlement agreement, the Coordinator should assist the Solicitor in developing the documents required for settlement. The settlement is typically documented by an agreement in principle followed by a consent decree, a legally binding document entered in the court that establishes the monetary amount to be paid to the trustees, specifies restoration actions to be implemented or both. Other specific details of the agreement also may be stipulated in the decree.

A global settlement, in which all claims are included and resolved, is often preferred by PRPs or agencies. Global settlements may include response and NRDAR damages claims, and include all agencies' interests. In such cases it is important to ensure that all BLM response and damages claims are sufficiently itemized and represented in supporting documents and negotiations.

3.6.5 Damages Claims in Bankruptcies

In some cases, a PRP may be in bankruptcy proceedings or file for bankruptcy during the NRDA activities. Bankruptcies require the filing of any claims against the PRP by a bar date that is set by the bankruptcy court. In order to recover any compensation for NRD claims, it is critical to file a Proof of Claim by this date or risk losing the ability to recover against the bankrupt PRP. Any potential claim should be discussed as quickly as possible with the Office of the Solicitor and the Department of Justice in order to determine if a claim needs to be filed with the bankruptcy court. Preparation of the claim and the proof of claim must be done with the Office of the Solicitor and DOJ. The bankruptcy process often is an accelerated process that requires development of a claim without the completion of an assessment. The Coordinator should ensure that the case Solicitor is central to any NRDAR activities involving bankruptcies.

3.6.6 Receiving Damages Claims from Settlement or Litigation

Once the settlement is concluded through a settlement agreement or a consent decree, or litigation is concluded, and the monetary damages are received through settlement or awarded by a court, an account should be established for the damages received. The DOI encourages trustee bureaus to place funds into interest-bearing accounts managed by the DOI that are subsequently disbursed according to trustee council decisions on restoration actions. Funds also may be placed in court registry or escrow accounts; however, these accounts may have maintenance fees and not be interest-bearing.

> Under CERCLA, all funds recovered for natural resource damage claims and assessment costs must be maintained in a separate, site-specific account to be used for reimbursement of assessment costs and actions described in the restoration plan. Any interest earned on restoration recovery accounts must be used only for restoration.

The specifics of the account differ depending on whether the Federal government, a State government, or an Indian tribe recover the funds. The DOI Restoration Fund has authorization to receive and maintain restoration recoveries in interest-bearing accounts and to disburse them as requested by trustee council resolutions. The recovered assessment costs from DOI appropriations are held in accounts separate from the recovered bureau assessment costs. The DOI

Restoration Fund may maintain recoveries jointly held by the DOI, and other Federal, State, and tribal co-trustees, by agreement.

Other Federal trustees may use a separate account in the U.S. Treasury; State trustees may use a separate account in the State treasury or an interest-bearing account payable in trust to the State trustee agency; and Indian tribes may use a separate account in the tribal treasury or an interest-bearing account payable in trust to the Indian tribe.

> Under OPA, all sums must be placed in a separate revolving trust account (15 CFR 990.65). Funds may be used to reimburse the trustees for past assessment costs and to implement the final restoration plan. Any interest earned on the account also must be used only for restoration. If co-trustees recover funds, a joint account may be created and an agreement may be developed to manage the account. The trustees must maintain appropriate records to document expenditures from the account. Any funds remaining in the account following the implementation of restoration must be deposited into the Oil Spill Liability Trust Fund.

3.6.7   Restoration Planning After Damages Receipt

After the Coordinator and co-trustees receive the damages from the PRP, the Coordinator begins to plan the actual restoration that the trustees will implement on the public's behalf. This planning process results in a draft Restoration Plan and environmental analysis, a public review, and a final document. The Restoration Plan describes how the Coordinator will use the damages received to restore resources and services. The Coordinator should use a portion of the recovered damages to fund the development and implementation of the Restoration Plan.

The Coordinator should follow the pre-claim restoration planning as closely as possible and base the contents of the Restoration Plan on the pre-claim planning that was done during the damages determination phase and described in the Report of Assessment. If the damages amount received is similar to the original claim, the details in pre-claim restoration planning may be carried over to the post-claim Restoration Plan and the Coordinator may propose to the public that the pre-claim plan be implemented. For some cases, the settlement consent decree or litigation document may specify certain restoration actions or place other restraints on post-claim planning. If the damages amount received is less than the original claim, some pre-claim planned actions or the scale of some actions may not be fully implemented. If the amount of damages received is less, the Coordinator should consider changes to the set of alternatives or adjustments to elements of the preferred alternative. The post-claim Restoration Plan will undergo public review, which could yield other restoration alternatives, and the Coordinator should take advantage of public input.

The plan should list alternatives for using the damages received and select the preferred alternative. The pre-claim evaluation criteria should be sufficient for post-claim planning. In addition, for each alternative, the plan should include project implementation details, monitoring and maintenance schedules, and criteria by which trustees will determine project success. For each project, trustees should identify a project goal, a set of quantifiable objective statements that address the goal, a set of parameters that will be monitored to assess project success, and a target value for each parameter that will be monitored. If HEA or REA were used to estimate the project scale, the metric used to set the scale for the project should be included as a monitoring parameter, if possible. Monitoring and evaluation are the only means by which the trustees can demonstrate to the public that they have fulfilled their mandate of protecting the public's natural resources.

3.6.8   National Environmental Policy Act (NEPA) and Other Requirements

The Coordinator should ensure that the Restoration Plan complies with applicable provisions of law, regulation, and policy. These include NEPA and the National Historic Preservation Act and others that may affect the nature of planned restoration actions.

It is DOI policy to comply with NEPA in providing the public an opportunity to comment on the restoration actions the Federal trustees propose, because they are Federal actions using funds received in the damages claim. Note that the steps of the NRDA process prior to the trustees' receipt of damages involve public review (e.g., the assessment plan) but they do not present NRDA alternatives. The Coordinator should ensure that the restoration plan is written according to NEPA requirements, which means to present reasonable alternatives of restoration actions and the environmental consequences of those actions. These requirements focus on selecting the most effective and least impacting actions to achieve restoration. Thus, the plan should include descriptions of the alternatives considered, the preferred alternative, and the evaluation process used to select it.

It may happen that actions that satisfy the trustees' restoration goals have already been evaluated through the NEPA public review and comment process in other existing plans, such as the BLM RMPs or interagency resource use plans. In such cases, the NEPA process regarding those actions might be deemed as completed, and the new formulation of alternatives may not be necessary. The Coordinator would then provide reference to and availability of these plans and the NEPA process when addressing the specific actions in the case Restoration Plan.

The NEPA process consists of three levels of analysis, depending on whether or not a restoration action could significantly affect the environment. The levels include categorical exclusion determination, the preparation of an environmental assessment/finding of no significant impact (EA/FONSI), or preparation of an environmental impact statement (EIS) (see DM 516 Chapter 11 for NEPA guidance for the BLM). If the EA determines that the environmental consequences of a restoration project might be significant, the Coordinator should prepare an EIS. An EIS involves a more detailed evaluation of the proposed action and alternatives.

The Coordinator may be able to categorically exclude a restoration or acquisition action from detailed environmental analysis if it meets certain criteria. The DOI and the BLM maintain lists of categorical exclusions (CX), and also lists of exceptions that would preclude an action from being categorically excluded (see 516 DM Chapter 2, Appendix 1, and Chapter 11). If a proposed restoration action fits into a CX and no exceptions apply, the trustees can proceed with the project without preparing an EA or EIS. If several DOI bureaus are co-trustees, they may use a CX from a bureau's list if it directly pertains to the action being considered. The BLM is currently revising its policies and procedures for compliance with NEPA and plans to create a number of new CXs (FR 71 (16):4159-4167, January 25, 2006).

If a proposed project is not categorically excluded, the trustees must prepare an EA to determine whether or not the project would significantly affect the environment. If the answer is no—that the project would not significantly affect the environment—then the trustees (or lead Federal agency among the trustees) issue a FONSI. The FONSI can address measures that the trustees will take to minimize potentially significant adverse effects. If the answer is yes—that the project would significantly affect the environment—then an EIS must be prepared.

In an EIS, the cumulative and induced impacts of multiple projects must be evaluated. A cumulative impacts analysis is intended to prevent a set of seemingly independent projects from adding up to be a significant problem. The public, other Federal agencies, and outside parties may provide input into the preparation of an EIS and comment on the draft EIS when it is completed. After a final EIS is prepared, the trustees prepare a public record of the decision that explains how the findings of the EIS, including the consideration of alternatives, were incorporated into the decision-making process.

NEPA evaluation can begin during the pre-claim restoration planning phase, since criteria used to screen and rank projects are relevant to consideration of environmental impacts. In addition, the public review requirements of NRDAR and NEPA can be combined, since documents that consider restoration alternatives, including the AP, the RCDP, and the restoration plan, are all made available for public comment. The final restoration plan or RCDP includes responses to public comments and a summary of changes made to the draft plan. After damages are awarded, a restoration plan is prepared to describe which proposed restoration projects will be implemented. This final plan can also describe how the NEPA requirements were addressed during the planning stages.

4. COOPERATIVE AGREEMENTS AND ASSESSMENTS WITH PRPS

4.1 INTRODUCTION

It may be possible for the Coordinator and co-trustees to reach a cooperative agreement with a PRP. Coordinators and co-trustees should periodically assess the receptiveness of the PRP to enter a cooperative agreement, because an agreement could become mutually advantageous at any point during NRDAR activities. PRP participation in the trustees' NRDAR process is not required, but is encouraged if trustee costs can be avoided or recovered and the agreement promotes an efficient assessment and acceptable terms for funding and participation can be negotiated.

PRP cooperation could range from granting the trustees a tolling agreement, which may extend the time in which the BLM has the authority to bring a damages claim, to providing up-front funding for a cooperative assessment, or something in between. The PRP's willingness to enter a cooperative agreement may depend on numerous factors: their own estimate of the damages and defenses to liability; the status and schedule of response activities at the site; the scope or schedule of the trustees' assessment; the PRP's financial ability and/or technical capabilities to conduct assessment or restoration; the PRP's openness to be bound by cooperative arrangement decisions; or other factors.

If a cooperative agreement is negotiated, the Coordinator, co-trustees, and the Office of the Solicitor should establish an MOU with the PRP to define the relationship. The MOU might include agreements on PRP funding and participation, and it might define the process that the parties to the MOU will follow to assess injuries and restoration needs. PRPs may be willing to enter into such an agreement because it allows them the ability to monitor assessment costs and participate in assessment decisions. Under statute, PRPs are also liable for all reasonable trustee assessment costs. Sometimes a PRP may offer up-front funding, but normally a PRP will periodically reimburse trustee costs.

If a cooperative agreement is not arranged, according to the regulations, the PRP may be involved in the trustees' NRDA during reviews of public NRDA documents (e.g., the AP, RCDP, and the Report of Assessment with its restoration plan) as well as after compilation of the damages claim, during negotiations toward settlement, or in discovery for litigation.

4.2 COOPERATIVE ASSESSMENTS

A cooperative PRP may be willing to participate in a cooperative assessment, and fund all or some of the trustees' assessment activities, enabling the BLM and co-trustees to avoid all or some NRDA costs. Cooperative assessments are likely to be more cost-effective and expedient than both parties conducting separate data collection, by eliminating duplicate efforts, allowing for agreements on technical issues like the extent of injuries, and promoting earlier focus on restoration. Sometimes PRPs may resort to conducting their own studies and analyses, internally or under contract, as an alternative to the trustees' NRDA.

Cooperative assessment could take various forms, such as PRP up-front funding or cost-sharing of a cooperatively designed assessment, PRP reimbursement for a trustee assessment, PRP conduct of the assessment with trustee oversight, or some other variation. A PRP could agree with trustee determinations of injury without extensive assessment, and cooperate on identifying mutually acceptable restoration actions. Participation could include data and information sharing, partial or full funding of data collection and analysis, consultation or involvement in developing and implementing methods and approaches, or providing expertise, equipment, or facilities.

4.3 FACTORS TO CONSIDER IN COOPERATIVE ASSESSMENTS

The Coordinator should note that cooperative assessments require careful management, because the objectives of the PRPs and the BLM may differ. The Coordinator should be aware of statute of limitation issues, and should secure a tolling agreement from the PRP when entering into an agreement. A tolling agreement, either as part of the MOU or as a separate document, suspends the clock on the statute of limitations while a cooperative assessment proceeds. Coordinators should seek input from and assist the Office of the Solicitor regarding MOA with PRPs to structure cooperative assessments, tolling agreements, and any other funding and participation agreements.

A PRP's goal is typically to eliminate liability quickly and cost-effectively, while the Coordinator's goal is to carry out statutory responsibilities to achieve restoration. The Coordinator should, therefore, conscientiously obtain enough information about the type, degree, and duration of the injuries and service losses to ensure that the public trust is protected and that the public is sufficiently compensated by the restoration. The Coordinator should be prepared to seek funding from internal sources for any studies that the PRP does not agree to fund within the trustees' assessment. In the end, the reasonable costs of assessment can be resolved at the time of settlement. Cooperating from a position of technical and legal strength in a cooperative assessment is just as important as in a litigated assessment. Progress made by the parties in agreeing to injuries, baseline conditions, service losses, damages, and other specific elements of the case should be formalized in legally-binding documentation. In a cooperative assessment, the PRP may pay for both the costs of the trustees' assessment work and the restoration actions deemed necessary by the assessment. The Coordinator should be prepared to encounter differences of opinion as to the need for particular assessment activities, the methods or techniques to be used for an assessment, and the particular metrics or endpoints that should be measured.

5. REFERENCES

Allen II, P.D., D.J. Chapman, and D. Lane. 2005. Scaling environmental restoration to offset injury using habitat equivalency analysis. Chapter 8 in *Economics and Ecological Risk Assessment, Applications to Watershed Management,* R.J.F. Bruins and M.T. Heberling (eds.). CRC Press, Boca Raton, FL, pp. 165-184.

Chapman, D., N. Iadanza, and T. Penn. 1998. Calculating Resource Compensation: An Application of the Service-to-Service Approach to the Blackbird Mine, Hazardous Waste Site. National Oceanic and Atmospheric Administration, Damage Assessment and Restoration Program, Technical Paper 97-1.

Dunford, R.W., T.C. Ginn, and W.H. Desvouges. 2004. The use of habitat equivalency analysis in natural resource damage assessments. *Ecological Economics.* 48:49-70.

Efroymson, R.A., M.E. Will, and G.W. Suter II. 1997a. Toxicological Benchmarks for Contaminants of Potential Concern for Effects on Soil and Litter Invertebrates and Heterotrophic Process: 1997 Revision. ES/ER/TM-126/R2. Prepared by Lockheed Martin Energy Systems, Inc. for the U.S. Department of Energy. November.

Efroymson, R.A., M.E. Will, G.W. Suter, and A.C. Wooten. 1997b. Toxicological Benchmarks for Screening Potential Contaminants of Concern for Effects on Terrestrial Plants: 1997 Revision. ES/ER/TM-85/R3. Prepared by Lockheed Martin Energy Systems, Inc. for the U.S. Department of Energy. November.

Ford, K. 2004. Risk Management Criteria for Metals at BLM Mining Sites, 2004 Revision. Technical Note 390, BLM/RS/ST-97/001+1703. Bureau of Land Management, Denver, CO.

Freeman, A.M. III. 1993. *The Measurement of Environmental and Resource Values: Theory and Methods.* (Resources for the Future, Washington, DC).

Kabata-Pendias, A. and H. Pendias. 1992. *Trace Elements in Soils and Plants.* CRC Press, Boca Raton, FL.

MacDonald, D.D., C.G. Ingersoll, and T.A. Berger. 2000. Development and evaluation of consensus-based sediment quality guidelines for freshwater ecosystems. *Archives of Environmental Contamination and Toxicology* 39:20-31.

NOAA. 1997. Scaling Compensatory Restoration Action: Guidance Document for Natural Resource Damage Assessment Under the Oil Pollution Act of 1990 Damage Assessment and Restoration Program. http://www.darp.noaa.gov/pdf/scaling.pdf.

NOAA. 2000. Habitat Equivalency Analysis: An Overview. Prepared by the Damage Assessment and Restoration Program, March 21, 1995. Revised October 4, 2000.

NOAA Coastal Services Center. 2004. Habitat Equivalency Analysis. http://www.csc.noaa.gov/coastal/economics/habitatequ.htm. Charleston, SC.

NOAA-DARP. 1996. Guidance Documents for Natural Resource Damage Assessment Under the Oil Pollution Act of 1990. CD-ROM. Developed by National Oceanic and Atmospheric Administration, Damage Assessment and Restoration Program. August.

Peacock, B. 1999. Habitat Equivalency Analysis: Conceptual Background and Hypothetical Example. April 30. National Park Service, Environmental Quality Division, Washington, DC.

Sperduto, Hebert, Donlan, and Thompson. 1999. "Injury Quantification and Restoration Scaling for Marine Birds Killed as a Result of the North Cape Oil Spill," (US Fish & Wildlife Service and Industrial Economics, MA, March).

Strange, E.M., P.D. Allen, D. Beltman, J. Lipton, D. Mills. 2004. The habitat-based replacement cost method for assessing monetary damages for fish resource injuries. *Fisheries* 29(7):17-23.

Strange, E.M., H. Galbraith, S. Bickel, D. Mills, D. Beltman, and J. Lipton. 2002. Determining ecological equivalence in service-to-service scaling of salt marsh restoration. *Environmental Management* 29:290-300.

U.S. EPA. 1987. Quality Criteria for Water 1986. EPA 440/5-86-001. U.S. Environmental Protection Agency, Washington, DC.

U.S. EPA. 2002. National Recommended Water Quality Criteria: 2002. EPA-822-R-02-047. U.S. Environmental Protection Agency Office of Water, Washington, DC. November.

Additional Guidance and Discussion of HEA/REA

Allen II, P.D., D.J. Chapman, and D. Lane. 2005. Scaling environmental restoration to offset injury using habitat equivalency analysis. Chapter 8 in *Economics and Ecological Risk Assessment, Applications to Watershed Management,* R.J.F. Bruins and M.T. Heberling (eds.). CRC Press, Boca Raton, FL, pp. 165-184.

Chapman, D., N. Iadanza, and T. Penn. 1998. Calculating Resource Compensation: An Application of the Service-to-Service Approach to the Blackbird Mine, Hazardous Waste Site. National Oceanic and Atmospheric Administration, Damage Assessment and Restoration Program, Technical Paper 97-1.

Dunford, T.C. Ginn, and W.H. Desvouges. 2004. The use of habitat equivalency analysis in natural resource damage assessments. *Ecological Economics* 48:49-70.

NOAA Coastal Services Center. 2004. Habitat Equivalency Analysis. http://www.csc.noaa.gov/coastal/economics/habitatequ.htm. Charleston, SC.

NOAA. 1997. Scaling Compensatory Restoration Action: Guidance Document for Natural Resource Damage Assessment Under the Oil Pollution Act of 1990 Damage Assessment and Restoration Program. http://www.darp.noaa.gov/pdf/scaling.pdf.

NOAA. 2000. Habitat Equivalency Analysis: An Overview. Prepared by the Damage Assessment and Restoration Program, March 21, 1995. Revised October 4, 2000.

Strange, E.M., H. Galbraith, S. Bickel, D. Mills, D. Beltman, and J. Lipton. 2002. Determining ecological equivalence in service-to-service scaling of salt marsh restoration. *Environmental Management* 29:290-300.

Strange, E.M., P.D. Allen, D. Beltman, J. Lipton, and D. Mills. 2004. The habitat-based replacement cost method for assessing monetary damages for fish resource injuries. *Fisheries* 29(7):17-23.

APPENDIX A

Legal References and Background Information

Legal underpinnings of NRDAR:

◆ The Trans-Alaska Pipeline Authorization Act (TAPAA) of 1973 (43 U.S.C. 1651)

◆ The Deepwater Ports Act (DPA) of 1974 (33 U.S.C. 1501, et seq.)

◆ The Federal Water Pollution Control Act (CWA) amendments of 1977 (33 U.S.C. 1251, et seq.)

◆ The Comprehensive Environmental Response, Compensation and Liability Act (CERCLA) of 1980 (42 U.S.C. 9601, et seq.)

◆ The Superfund Amendments and Reauthorization Act (SARA) of 1986 (42 U.S.C. 9601, et seq., amending CERCLA)

◆ The Marine Protection, Research, and Sanctuaries Act (MPRSA) amendments of 1988 (33 U.S.C. 1401, et seq.)

◆ The National Park System Resources Protection Act (NPSRA) of 1990 (Public Law 101-337)

◆ The Oil Pollution Act (OPA) of 1990 (33 U.S.C. 2701, et seq.).

Cases that helped to define the application of statutes and regulations to NRDAR sites:

◆ New Bedford Harbor, Massachusetts (*In re: Acushnet River and New Bedford Harbor*: 675 F. Supp. 22; 712 F. Supp. 994, 1010, 1019; 722 F. Supp. 888, 893; and *United States v. AVX Corp.*, 962 F.2d 108).

◆ Clark Fork, Montana (*Montana v. Atlantic Richfield*, 273 F. Supp. 2d 1159).

◆ Prince William Sound, Alaska (*In re: Exxon Valdez*: 767 F. Supp. 1509; 104 F.3d 1196; 229 F.3d 790; 270 F.3d 1215; and *Alaska Sport Fishing Ass'n v. Exxon Corp.* 34 F.3d 769).

◆ Los Angeles, California (*United States v. Montrose Chemical Corp. of California*: 22 ELR 21327; 25 ELR 20703, 20809; 788 F. Supp. 1485; 827 F. Supp. 1453; 835 F. Supp. 534; 132 F.3d 90).

◆ Coeur d'Alene, Idaho (*Idaho v. Bunker Hill Co.*: 16 ELR 20715; 635 F. Supp. 665; *Coeur D'Alene Tribe v. ASARCO Inc.*, 280 F. Supp. 1094; Sept. 3, 2003 unpublished decision; and *United States v. ASARCO Inc.*: 29 ELR 20188; 214 F.3d 1104).

APPENDIX B

Example Supplemental Cost Documentation Forms

The cost tracking forms in Appendix B are for use by the Coordinator and other staff involved in NRDAR cases. These forms have been developed by the DOI NRDAR Program for use by bureau practitioners; their use or the use of analogous forms should constitute sufficient cost documentation when used to support official BLM financial records (see Section 2.5). The Coordinator should evaluate whether these forms are necessary to document case costs for recovery. These forms may be necessary to supplement official cost documentation records of BLM, like the Management Information System, if cost recovery efforts require additional information. If used, the forms must be case-specific, and the labor cost form should be completed separately by each involved employee. These forms may require the attachment of official documents that show the BLM payment of the costs listed.

Narrative Instructions for Completing Cost Documentation Forms

Table of Contents

Cost Documentation Forms Background

The NRDAR Program has developed a set of standardized forms, in Microsoft Excel format, for DOI NRDAR practitioner use in documenting costs and compiling cost documentation reports associated with NRDAR projects. These NRDAR Program cost documentation forms have been adapted from the U.S. Coast Guard National Pollution Funds Center's series CG-5136 forms (*i.e.,* "Pollution Incident Daily Resource Reports") for documenting oil spill response expenses pursuant to the Oil Pollution Act of 1990 and display all of the same data elements as the CG-5136 series of forms. All of the specific data elements included on the CG-5136 series of forms are included on the DOI NRDAR Program forms. No new data elements have been developed for the DOI NRDAR Program Forms.

Use of these forms presumes a basic working knowledge of the Microsoft Excel spreadsheet program.

These NRDAR Program cost documentation forms include the following seven forms, which together comprise a cost documentation package:

Summary Cost Report: for use in summarizing labor costs, travel costs, contract costs, purchases/expendables costs and government equipment costs.

Labor Cost Report: for use in compiling and documenting project-related labor costs.

Labor Cost Report (last page): for use in compiling applicable indirect/overhead rates associated with labor costs.

Travel Cost Report: for use in compiling and documenting project-related, official government travel costs.

Contracts Cost Report: for use in compiling and documenting project-related contract costs.

Purchases/Expendables Cost Report: for use in compiling and documenting costs associated with project-related purchases and expendable supplies (*e.g.,* laboratory sample jars, safety equipment).

Government Equipment Cost Report: for use in compiling and documenting costs associated with the project-related use of government equipment (*e.g.,* truck, boat, all-terrain vehicle, bulldozer).

Use of these forms by DOI NRDAR practitioners for documentation of costs can be expected to provide the following advantages:

1

1. the forms are currently under review by the U.S. Coast Guard National Pollution Funds Center as an "Approved Alternative Record Keeping System." With this approval, these forms can be substituted for the CG-5136 series forms.

2. the forms are versatile and can be used for cost documentation for NRDAR projects under CWA, OPA and CERCLA.

3. the forms are in Microsoft Excel format with automatic mathematical calculations built into the form reducing the opportunity for simple arithmetic errors.

4. the forms include the automatic calculation of program-wide indirect and overhead rates and provide for the inclusion and calculation of specific bureau/office indirect and overhead rates as appropriate.

5. use of these forms will result in consistent, defensible and easily understood cost documentation.

It is generally recommended that project-related costs be compiled on a fiscal year (FY) basis (*i.e.*, October 1 through September 30) when using these forms. Certain indirect and overhead rates applicable to NRDAR projects, both Program-wide and bureau-specific, can vary over time and complicate cost documentation, however, these rates typically remain consistent within a fiscal year.

Summary Cost Report

This form summarizes the five different categories of recoverable costs associated with NRDAR projects: labor; travel; contracts; purchases/expendables; and, government equipment.

Instructions

The Summary Cost Report form asks for certain project-specific identifying information at the top of the form. This project-specific identifying information is (or should be) consistent throughout the six different forms within a single cost documentation package and, therefore, can be copied and pasted into the other forms as needed. The following information should be completed:

Incident/Site name, location: enter the name and location of the oil spill or hazardous material release incident or the uncontrolled hazardous waste site (*e.g.*, ABC pipeline oil spill, Norfolk, VA).

Incident/Site FPN or CERCLA ID no.: enter the unique identifying number for incident's Federal Project Number (FPN) or the site's CERCLA ID number (*e.g.*, FPN X-12345).

Inclusive dates of billing: enter the date range for which this particular cost documentation applies (*e.g.*, 10/1/03 - 9/30/04).

2

Billing bureau/office: enter the name of the bureau/office to which this cost documentation applies (*e.g.*, Bureau of Land Management, Chesapeake Bay Field Office).

Billing bureau/office contact: enter name, title, mailing address, phone number and fax number of the contact person assembling the cost documentation or the person most familiar with the cost documentation in case questions arise later.

The following information, specific to this form, should also be completed:

Cost: for each of the five different categories of expenses (*i.e.*, labor, travel, contracts, purchases/expendables and government equipment), enter the total cost associated with that category. These numbers are derived from the more detailed associated reports for each of the five categories.

Detailed Report attached (YES or NO): indicate, with a "yes" or a "no", whether a detailed report on any of the five different categories of expenses is attached to this cost documentation package.

Labor Cost Report

This form reports NRDAR project-related labor costs on a daily basis. The cost of labor is based on an hourly pay rate.

Because labor costs are reported on a daily basis and, therefore, requiring more overall form space to report these expenses, multiple pages are typically required for a Labor Cost Report. Two versions of the Labor Cost Report are provided to accommodate the more extensive reporting required for daily labor: 1) a version intended to be used as a continuation page, called the "Labor Cost Report" that does not include the applicable indirect rate calculations and, 2) a version intended to be used as the last page in a Labor Cost Report, called the "Labor Cost Report (last page)" that includes the applicable indirect rate calculations.

Instructions

Complete the project-specific identifying information at the top of the form following the instructions provided in the Instructions section for the Summary Cost Report. This information should be consistent throughout all the forms comprising a single cost documentation package.

The following information, specific to this form should also be completed:

Are time & attendance worksheets attached? (YES or NO): indicate, with a "yes" or a "no", whether or not time & attendance worksheets or other timekeeping records are attached as supporting documentation. If formal timekeeping records are attached as supporting documentation, remember to redact Privacy Act-applicable information (*e.g.*, SSN) before releasing this documentation.

If YES, how many are attached? indicate how many pages of timekeeping records are

3

attached as supporting documentation to this report.

Employee name (last, first): enter the name of the employee (as last name, first name) for whom this report is documenting the labor expenses.

Date of activity: enter the date that the labor costs being reported were worked.

Pay grade: enter the pay grade or labor category of the employee whose labor costs are being reported (*e.g.*, O4, E5, GS12).

Activity code(s): enter the appropriate activity code or codes that apply to the labor costs being reported.

The NRDAR Program has developed two-tiered standard program activity codes for use in describing program-related labor activities. These NRDAR Program activity codes correspond with Departmental Activity-Based Cost Accounting activity categories and NRDAR Program case milestones.

These activity codes are listed below:

1.0   Assessment
      1.1   Preassessment activities
      1.2   Assessment planning
      1.3   Assessment implementation
      1.4   Settlement negotiations
      1.5   Case management
2.0   Restoration
      2.1   Restoration planning
      2.2   Restoration implementation
      2.3   Restoration monitoring
      2.4   Restoration management
3.0   Litigation

These activity codes are arranged into two tiers based on complexity to provide flexibility in reporting activities. Use the first tier codes (*i.e.*, 1.0, 2.0, 3.0) when only a general level of activity reporting is desired. Use the second tier codes (*i.e.*, 1.1, 1.2, 1.3, 1.4, 1.5, 2.1, 2.2, 2.3, 2.4) when more detailed activity reporting is desired.

No. of hours: enter the number of labor hours being reported. If fractional hours are being reported, these should be entered as a decimal number (*e.g.*, 1.5 for 1 hour and 30 minutes).

Pay rate per hour: enter the hourly pay rate associated with the labor hours being reported. This hourly pay rate should also include the proportional benefits associated with the standard hourly pay rate. Within the Department of the Interior, benefits can range between 10% and 30% of an employee's standard pay rate depending upon a variety

4

of factors specific to each employee.

Cost: Within each row on the form, "Cost" is automatically calculated by the spreadsheet by multiplying "No. of hours" by "Pay rate per hour."

Sub-Total of direct labor cost: the "Sub-Total of direct labor cost" is automatically calculated by the spreadsheet.

Remarks: enter any amplifying or clarifying information considered important to this report.

Labor Cost Report Form (last page)

This form is intended to be the final page of a Labor Cost Report. This form differs from the other Labor Cost Report form by including: 1) a line item for the calculation of the Department of the Interior Headquarters indirect rate of 16.84% of labor costs; and, 2) two optional line items for the calculation of applicable Bureau/Office indirect rates.

Instructions

Complete the project-specific identifying information at the top of the form following the instructions provided in the Instructions section for the Summary Cost Report. This information should be consistent throughout all the forms comprising a single cost documentation package.

The following information, specific to this form should also be completed:

Bureau/Office indirect rate (@ xx% of direct labor cost): if your bureau/office charges an indirect or overhead rate associated with labor costs, enter that rate here and adjust the formula in the Microsoft Excel spreadsheet to include this calculation in the final total labor cost.

Bureau/Office indirect rate (@ xx% of direct labor cost): if your bureau/office charges an indirect or overhead rate associated with labor costs, enter that rate here and adjust the formula in the Microsoft Excel spreadsheet to include this calculation in the final total labor cost.

Total labor cost: the "Total labor cost" is automatically calculated by the spreadsheet. This "Total labor cost" number should be entered into the associated Summary Cost Report.

Travel Cost Report

This form reports NRDAR project-related travel costs on a trip-by-trip basis and calculates associated indirect and/or overhead rates if applicable.

Instructions

5

Complete the project-specific identifying information at the top of the form following the instructions provided in the Instructions section for the Summary Cost Report. This information should be consistent throughout all the forms comprising a single cost documentation package.

The following information, specific to this form, should also be completed:

Were Travel Authorizations (DI-1020) issued? (YES or NO): indicate, with a "yes" or a "no", whether or not Travel Authorizations (*i.e.*, Department of the Interior form DI-1020) were issued for the travel costs being reported.

If YES, are copies attached (YES or NO): indicate, with a "yes" or a "no", whether or not copies of Travel Authorization forms are attached as supporting documentation to this report.

If YES, how many are attached?: indicate how many pages of Travel Authorization forms are attached as supporting documentation to this report.

Are liquidated Travel Vouchers (SF-1012) attached? (YES or NO): indicate, with a "yes" or a "no", whether or not liquidated (*i.e.*, supervisor-approved and paid) Travel Vouchers (Standard Form SF-1020) are attached to this report as supporting documentation. If liquidated Travel Vouchers are attached as supporting documentation, remember to redact Privacy Act-applicable information (*e.g.*, SSN, credit card numbers) before releasing this documentation.

Name of traveler (last, first): enter the name of the employee (as last name, first name) for whom this report is documenting the travel costs.

Date(s) of travel: enter the date or dates that the travel costs were incurred (*e.g.*, 11/1/03 - 11/2/03).

Travel Authorization Number: enter the Travel Authorization Number associated with the travel costs being reported.

Issued by: enter the name initials of bureau/office that issued the Travel Authorization associated with the travel costs being reported (*e.g.*, BIA/WRO, FWS/R2, DOI/SOL).

Cost: enter the total travel cost for the trip being reported.

Sub-Total travel cost: the "Sub-Total travel cost" is automatically calculated by the spreadsheet.

Bureau/office indirect rate, if applicable (@ xx% of travel cost): if your bureau/office charges an indirect or overhead rate associated with travel costs, enter that rate here and adjust the formula in the Microsoft Excel spreadsheet to include this calculation in the final total travel cost.

6

Bureau/office indirect rate, if applicable (@ xx% of travel cost): if your bureau/office charges an indirect or overhead rate associated with travel costs, enter that rate here and adjust the formula in the Microsoft Excel spreadsheet to include this calculation in the final total travel cost.

Total travel cost: the "Total travel cost" is automatically calculated by the spreadsheet. This "Total travel cost" number should be entered into the associated Summary Cost Report.

Remarks: enter any amplifying or clarifying information considered important to this report.

Contracts Cost Report

This form reports NRDAR project-related contract costs and calculates associated indirect and/or overhead rates if applicable.

Instructions

Complete the project-specific identifying information at the top of the form following the instructions provided in the Instructions section for the Summary Cost Report. This information should be consistent throughout all the forms comprising a single cost documentation package.

The following information, specific to this form should also be completed:

Were Purchase Orders (DI-52) issued? (YES or NO): indicate, with a "yes" or a "no", whether or not Purchase Order forms (*i.e.*, Department of the Interior DI-52 forms) were issued for the contracts in this report.

If YES, are copies attached? (YES or NO): indicate, with a "yes" or a "no", whether or not copies of these Purchase Orders are attached to this report.

If YES, how many are attached?: indicate how many pages of Purchase Order forms are attached as supporting documentation to this report.

Name: enter the name of the contract or contractor.

Purchase Order or Contractor no.: enter the Purchase Order number or Contractor number associated with this contractor.

Cost: enter the total cost for this contract.

Sub-Total contracts cost: the "Sub-Total contracts cost" is automatically calculated by the spreadsheet.

7

Bureau/Office indirect rate, if applicable (@ xx% of contracts cost): if your bureau/office charges an indirect or overhead rate associated with contract costs, enter that rate here and adjust the formula in the Microsoft Excel spreadsheet to include this calculation in the final total contract cost.

Bureau/Office indirect rate, if applicable (@ xx% of contracts cost): if your bureau/office charges an indirect or overhead rate associated with contract costs, enter that rate here and adjust the formula in the Microsoft Excel spreadsheet to include this calculation in the final total contract cost.

Total contracts cost: the "Total contracts cost" is automatically calculated by the spreadsheet. This "Total contracts cost" number should be entered into the associated Summary Cost Report.

Remarks: enter any amplifying or clarifying information considered important to this report.

Purchases/Expendables Cost Report

This form reports NRDAR project-related purchases and expendable supplies costs and calculates associated indirect and/or overhead rates if applicable.

Instructions

Complete the project-specific identifying information at the top of the form following the instructions provided in the Instructions section for the Summary Cost Report. This information should be consistent throughout all the forms comprising a single cost documentation package.

The following information, specific to this form, should also be completed:

Were any Purchase Orders (DI-52) completed? (YES or NO): indicate, with a "yes" or a "no", whether or not Purchase Order forms (*i.e.*, Department of the Interior DI-52 forms) were issued for the purchases and/or expendable supplies in this report.

If YES, how many were completed?: indicate how many Purchase Order forms (*i.e.*, Department of the Interior DI-52 forms) were completed for purchases and/or expendable supplies in this report.

If YES, are they attached? (YES or NO): indicate, with a "yes" or a "no", whether or not the completed Purchase Order forms (*i.e.*, Department of the Interior DI-52 forms) are attached as supporting documentation to this report.

If YES, how many are attached?: indicate how many pages of Purchase Order forms are attached as supporting documentation to this report.

Description of item: briefly describe the purchase or expendable supply item (*e.g.*,

8

laboratory sample jars, safety supplies [gloves]).

Purchase Order no.: enter the Purchase Order number associated with this purchase or expendable supply item.

Cost: enter the total cost for this item.

Sub-Total purchases/expendables cost: the "Sub-Total purchases/expendables cost" is automatically calculated by the spreadsheet.

Bureau/Office indirect rate, if applicable (@ xx% of contracts cost): if your bureau/office charges an indirect or overhead rate associated with purchases and expendable supply costs, enter that rate here and adjust the formula in the Microsoft Excel spreadsheet to include this calculation in the final total purchases/expendables cost.

Bureau/Office indirect rate, if applicable (@ xx% of contracts cost): if your bureau/office charges an indirect or overhead rate associated with purchases and expendable supply costs, enter that rate here and adjust the formula in the Microsoft Excel spreadsheet to include this calculation in the final total purchases/expendables cost.

Total purchases/expendables cost: the "Total purchases/expendables cost" is automatically calculated by the spreadsheet. This "Total purchases/expendables cost" number should be entered into the associated Summary Cost Report.

Remarks: enter any amplifying or clarifying information considered important to this report.

Government Equipment Cost Report

This form reports NRDAR project-related costs for the use of government-owned equipment and calculates associated indirect and/or overhead rates if applicable.

Instructions

Complete the project-specific identifying information at the top of the form following the instructions provided in the Instructions section for the Summary Cost Report. This information should be consistent throughout all the forms comprising a single cost documentation package.

The following information, specific to this form, should also be completed:

Item description: briefly describe the item of government equipment used (*e.g.*, pickup truck, boat, bulldozer).

Rate basis (*e.g.*, hourly, daily, weekly): describe the basis used for charging equipment costs (*e.g.*, hourly, daily, weekly).

9

No. of units: enter the number of units for which the equipment was utilized, defined in terms of the rate basis (*i.e.*, number of hours, number of days, number of weeks).

Rate per unit ($): enter the rate charged per unit. It can be helpful to attach a copy of your bureau's/office's standard rate table for government equipment or a computation showing how the rate was derived.

Rate charge ($): enter the rate per unit multiplied by the number of units.

Non-Rate charges ($): enter the total charges related to the equipment usage not charged on a per unit basis (*i.e.*, mileage, fuel, setup/takedown charges).

Total cost: enter the sum of the "Rate charge" and the "Non-Rate charges" for the use of this particular item of government equipment.

Sub-Total equipment cost: the "Sub-Total equipment cost" is automatically calculated by the spreadsheet.

Bureau/Office indirect rate, if applicable (@ xx% of contracts cost): if your bureau/office charges an indirect or overhead rate associated with the use of government-owned equipment, enter that rate here and adjust the formula in the Microsoft Excel spreadsheet to include this calculation in the final total government equipment cost.

Bureau/Office indirect rate, if applicable (@ xx% of contracts cost): if your bureau/office charges an indirect or overhead rate associated with the use of government-owned equipment, enter that rate here and adjust the formula in the Microsoft Excel spreadsheet to include this calculation in the final total government equipment cost.

Total equipment cost: the "Total equipment cost" is automatically calculated by the spreadsheet. This "Total equipment cost" number should be entered into the associated Summary Cost Report.

Remarks: enter any amplifying or clarifying information considered important to this report.

10

Bureau of Land Management — NRDAR Case Travel Costs

Page ____ of ____

Employee Name

Pay Series/Grade/Step

Employee Office Name

Case/Site Name

Case/Site Numerical Identifier

NRDAR Process Phase

Travel Dates	Office Code/	Case SIPC Code	Travel Voucher Number	Total Cost	Destination	Purpose of Travel

Certification: I certify that the travel posted is accurate for the work performed. I certify that the statements I have made on this form and all attachments are true, accurate, and complete. I acknowledge that any knowingly false or misleading statement may be punishable by fine or imprisonment or both under the law.

Employee's Signature ____ Date ____ Supervisor's Signature ____ Date ____

Bureau of Land Management — NRDAR Daily Case Labor Costs

Page _____ of _____

Employee Name

Employee Office Name

Pay Series/Grade/Step

Case//site Name

Case/Project/site Numerical Identifier

NRDAR Process Phase

Date	Pay period	Office Code/ Sub-activity	Case SIPC Code	Pay Rate/hr	Hours Worked	Total Daily Cost	Description of Work

Certification: I certify that this information is accurate for the work performed. I certify that the statements I have made on this form and all attachments are true, accurate, and complete. I acknowledge that any knowingly false or misleading statement may be punishable by fine or imprisonment or both under the law.

Employee's Signature	Date	Supervisor's Signature	Date

| Bureau of Land Management | | | | NRDAR Case Contracts/Supplies/Equipment Costs | | | Page _____ of _____ |

Purchasing Employee Name

Pay Series/Grade/Step

Employee Office Name

Case/Site Name

Case/Site Numerical Identifier

NRDAR Process Phase

Purchase Date	Office Code/Sub-activity	Purchase Order Number	Case SIPC Code	Total Cost	Description of Purchased Item	Number Purchased	Reason for Purchase

Certification: I certify that the travel posted is accurate for the work performed. I certify that the statements I have made on this form and all attachments are true, accurate, and complete. I acknowledge that any knowingly false or misleading statement may be punishable by fine or imprisonment or both under the law.

Employee's Signature   Date   Supervisor's Signature   Date

U.S. DOI Bureau of Land Management	Page 1 of 1
Natural Resource Damage Assessment & Restoration Program	
Summary Cost Report	(rev. 1/2006)

Incident/Site name, location:
Incident/Site FPN or CERCLA ID no.:
Inclusive dates of billing:
Billing bureau/office:
Billing bureau/office contact:

SUMMARY REPORT			
Expense category	Cost	Detailed Report attached? (YES or NO)	Office use
Labor			
Travel			
Contracts			
Purchases/Expendables			
Government equipment			

Total costs: **$0.00**

	**U.S. DOI Bureau of Land Management** **Natural Resource Damage Assessment & Restoration Program** **Labor Cost Report**	Page _ of _ (rev. 1/2006)

Incident/Site name, location:

Incident/Site FPN or CERCLA ID no.:

Inclusive dates of billing:

Billing bureau/office:

Billing bureau/office contact:

Are time & attendance worksheets attached? (YES or NO):

If YES, how many are attached?

LABOR REPORT

Employee name (last, first)/ Date of activity	Pay grade	Activity code(s)[1]	No. of hours	Pay rate per hour	Cost	Office use
					$0.00	
					$0.00	
					$0.00	
					$0.00	
					$0.00	
					$0.00	
					$0.00	
					$0.00	
					$0.00	
					$0.00	
					$0.00	
					$0.00	
					$0.00	
					$0.00	
					$0.00	
					$0.00	
					$0.00	
					$0.00	
					$0.00	
					$0.00	
					$0.00	
continued on next page						
				Sub-Total of direct labor cost:	**$0.00**	

[1] Activity Code key:

1.0: Assessment	2.0: Restoration
1.1: Preassessment activities	2.1: Restoration planning
1.2: Assessment planning	2.2: Restoration implementation
1.3: Assessment implementation	2.3: Restoration monitoring
1.4: Settlement negotiation	2.4: Restoration management
1.5: Case management	3.0: Litigation

Remarks:

U.S. DOI Bureau of Land Management	Page _ of _
Natural Resource Damage Assessment & Restoration Program	
Labor Cost Report	

Incident/Site name, location:

Incident/Site FPN or CERCLA ID no.:

Inclusive dates of billing:

Billing bureau/office:
Billing bureau/office contact:

Are time & attendance worksheets attached? (YES or NO):
If YES, how many are attached?

LABOR REPORT   (rev. 1/2006)

Employee name (last, first)/ Date of activity	Pay grade	Activity code(s)[1]	No. of hours	Pay rate per hour	Cost	Office use
					$0.00	
					$0.00	
					$0.00	
					$0.00	
					$0.00	
					$0.00	
					$0.00	
					$0.00	
					$0.00	
					$0.00	
					$0.00	
					$0.00	
					$0.00	
					$0.00	
					$0.00	
					$0.00	
					$0.00	
					$0.00	
					$0.00	

Sub-Total of direct labor cost:	$0.00
Bureau/Office indirect rate #1, if applicable (@ xx% of direct labor cost):	
Bureau/Office indirect rate #2, if applicable (@ xx% of direct labor cost):	
Dept. of the Interior Headquarters indirect rate (@ 16.84% of direct labor cost):	$0.00

	Total labor cost:	$0.00

			Remarks:
[1] Activity Code key:			
1.0: Assessment	2.0: Restoration		
1.1: Preassessment activities	2.1: Restoration planning		
1.2: Assessment planning	2.2: Restoration implementation		
1.3: Assessment implementation	2.3: Restoration monitoring		
1.4: Settlement negotiation	2.4: Restoration management		
1.5: Case management	3.0: Litigation		

	U.S. DOI Bureau of Land Management Natural Resource Damage Assessment & Restoration Program Travel Cost Report	Page _ of _ (rev. 1/2006)

Incident/Site name, location:

Incident/Site FPN or CERCLA ID no.:

Inclusive dates of billing:

Billing bureau/office:
Billing bureau/office contact:

Were Travel Authorizations (DI-1020) issued? (YES or NO):

If YES, are copies attached? (YES or NO):

If YES, how many are attached?

Are liquidated Travel Vouchers (SF-1012) attached? (YES or NO):

If YES, how many are attached?

TRAVEL REPORT

Name of traveler (last, first)	Date(s) of travel	Travel Authorization Number	Issued by	Cost	Office use

Sub-Total of travel cost:	$0.00	
Bureau/Office indirect rate #1, if applicable (@ xx% of travel cost):		
Bureau/Office indirect rate #2, if applicable (@ xx% of travel cost):		
Total travel cost:	**$0.00**	

Remarks:

U.S. DOI Bureau of Land Management
Natural Resource Damage Assessment & Restoration Program
Contracts Cost Report

Page _ of _

(rev. 1/2006)

Incident/Site name, location:

Incident/Site FPN or CERCLA ID no.:

Inclusive dates of billing:

Billing bureau/office:
Billing bureau/office contact:

Were Purchase Orders (DI-52) issued? (YES or NO):

If YES, are copies attached? (YES or NO):

If YES, how many are attached?

CONTRACTS REPORT

Name	Purchase Order or Contractor no.	Cost	Office use

	Cost
Sub-Total of contracts cost:	$0.00
Bureau/Office indirect rate #1, if applicable (@ xx% of contracts cost):	
Bureau/Office indirect rate #2, if applicable (@ xx% of contracts cost):	
Total contracts cost:	$0.00

Remarks:

|  | **U.S. DOI Bureau of Land Management**
Natural Resource Damage Assessment & Restoration Program

Purchases/Expendables Cost Report | Page _
of _

(rev.
1/2006) |

Incident/Site name, location:

Incident/Site FPN or CERCLA ID no.:

Inclusive dates of billing:

Billing bureau/office:

Billing bureau/office contact:

Were any Purchase Orders (DI-52) completed? (YES or NO):

If YES, how many were completed:

If YES, are they attached? (YES or NO):

If YES, how many are attached:

PURCHASES/EXPENDABLES REPORT			
Description of item	Purchase Order no.	Cost	Office use
	Sub-Total of purchases/expendables cost:	$0.00	
	Bureau/Office indirect rate #1, if applicable (@ xx% of purchases/expendables cost):		
	Bureau/Office indirect rate #2, if applicable (@ xx% of purchases/expendables cost):		
	Total purchases/expendables cost:	**$0.00**	

	U.S. DOI Bureau of Land Management	Page _ of _
	Natural Resource Damage Assessment & Restoration Program	
	Government Equipment Cost Report	(rev. 1/2006)

Incident/Site name, location:

Incident/Site FPN or CERCLA ID no.:

Inclusive dates of billing:

Billing bureau/office:

Billing bureau/office contact:

GOVERNMENT EQUIPMENT REPORT

Item description	Rate basis (e.g., hourly, daily, weekly)	No. of units	Rate per unit ($)	Rate charge ($)	Non-Rate charges ($)	Total cost	Office use
				$0.00		$0.00	
				$0.00		$0.00	
				$0.00		$0.00	
				$0.00		$0.00	
				$0.00		$0.00	
				$0.00		$0.00	
				$0.00		$0.00	
				$0.00		$0.00	
				$0.00		$0.00	
				$0.00		$0.00	
				$0.00		$0.00	
				$0.00		$0.00	
				$0.00		$0.00	
				$0.00		$0.00	
				$0.00		$0.00	
				$0.00		$0.00	
				$0.00		$0.00	
				$0.00		$0.00	
				$0.00		$0.00	

Sub-Total of government equipment cost:	$0.00
Bureau/Office indirect rate #1, if applicable (@ xx% of government equipment cost):	
Bureau/Office indirect rate #2, if applicable (@ xx% of government equipment cost):	
Total government equipment cost:	**$0.00**

Remarks:

APPENDIX C

Natural Resource Injury Scoping Report

It is the BLM policy to complete a natural resource injury scoping (NRIS) report for sites where the BLM makes a determination that a CERCLA or OPA response (removal or remedial) action may be warranted. This report documents the results of the natural resource injury scoping process. The report indicates whether injuries to the BLM resources or losses of services have occurred or are suspected, caused by a release of hazardous substances or an oil spill, and whether they can be restored from the response actions. If injuries or losses have occurred or are suspected, the report should list the specific resources thought to be potentially injured or the services lost. If specific resources or losses are identified, the actions thought necessary to restore them within the response action also should be identified. The report should be completed prior to the time when removal action needs are planned, and it should be placed in the case file and AR. The report should be signed by the Coordinator and the District/Field Office Manager. Other agencies that may have resource interests at the site should be listed, as well as known PRPs.

If further NRDAR activities are anticipated the Coordinator and the other involved DOI bureaus should begin the designation process for the DOI Authorized Official.

NRDAR Injury Scoping Report Form

1. Site Name/Location: **Report Date:**

_____ / _____

2. BLM Coordinator/Office:

(Print) _____ (Sign) _____

3. Signature of BLM Manager Verifying Injury Scoping Completion:

(Print)_____ (Sign) _____

4. Site/Setting/Description:

_____

_____

5. Description of CERCLA Release (what, where, toxicity, persistence):

_____

_____

6.   Y __ / N __   Is the BLM taking CERCLA or OPA response actions?

7. Natural Resource Injury Scoping:

_____ a. No resource injury suspected to resources

_____ b. Injury suspected for potentially affected resources

8. Natural Resources/Services Potentially Injured/Lost (list/briefly describe injury/loss):

_____

_____

9. Description of restoration needs by injured resource/lost service:

_____

_____

10. Other trustee agencies and resource interests:

_____

_____

11. Potentially Responsible Party (PRP) information:

_____

APPENDIX D

Determination Details of Resource and Habitat Injury

Surface Water – Aquatic Life Criteria

In determining injury to surface water, the Coordinator should compare measured concentrations of contaminants to the Federal and State criteria for water quality that have been designated to protect aquatic life (generally referred to as aquatic life criteria, or ALC). Pursuant to Section 304 of the CWA, EPA establishes national recommended ambient water quality criteria that are generally applicable to the waters of the United States (U.S. EPA, 2002). Numerous States and tribes have established similar water quality criteria.

Certain States have also designated water quality criteria for the protection of humans who consume aquatic organisms. These water quality criteria are intended to ensure that fish do not accumulate concentrations of substances from the water that would adversely affect the health of humans who ingest the fish.

Surface water – Drinking water

The Coordinator should use EPA drinking water standards in determining injury to surface waters used for drinking. The EPA, pursuant to the Safe Drinking Water Act, established three kinds of drinking water standards based on total recoverable metals. The maximum contaminant levels (MCLs) are the highest level of a contaminant that is allowed in drinking water from a public supplier. The MCL goals (MCLGs) are non-enforceable health goals that are set at levels at which no known or anticipated adverse effects to human health occur and which allow an adequate margin of safety. The Secondary Drinking Water Regulations (SDWRs) are also non-enforceable Federal guidelines regarding cosmetic effects (such as skin or tooth discoloration) or aesthetic effects (such as taste, odor, or color) of drinking water. Trustees can use MCLs and SDWRs to assess injuries to drinking water services.

Numerous States also have established standards to measure biotic or ecological integrity, to protect wildlife, and to protect human health for municipal or domestic water supply use. Such standards can be used to assess injuries to surface water.

Sediments

The Coordinator should refer to various contamination guidelines in determining sediment injuries. EPA has not developed relevant criteria to protect aquatic biota or wildlife from contaminants in sediments, and regulatory standards have not been promulgated. Various Federal, State, and provincial agencies in North America have developed numerical sediment quality guidelines, and sediment toxicity tests using a variety of approaches to assess the quality of freshwater and marine sediments. The approaches that have been selected by individual jurisdictions differ based on the ecological receptors considered, the degree of protection afforded, the geographic area to which the values are intended to apply, and the intended uses of the values.

These sediment quality guidelines cannot be applied as standards in a regulatory sense, but injury to sediments may be demonstrated if concentrations in the sediments are sufficient to cause injury to other resources, or if sediments are a pathway of injury. In this way, guidelines can be used as additional scientific evidence in evaluating potential injuries to biological resources that rely upon sediments.

Ground water

The Coordinator should use the national drinking water standards in determining injury to ground water resources. Ground water resources may also be injured if other natural resources are injured as a result of exposure to contaminated ground water. For example, if ground water discharges to surface water at a seep, spring, or gaining section of a stream, surface water may be injured via a ground water pathway. Trustees may evaluate injury to ground water by comparing measured concentrations of hazardous substances in samples collected from seeps or springs flowing from ground water to surface water quality criteria.

Soils

The Coordinator should refer to the regulatory definitions of injury in determining injury to soils. It also may be useful to compare contaminant data in soils to toxicological benchmarks indicative of injuries to soil invertebrates and plants. The Department of Energy (DOE) has developed a set of toxicological benchmarks for effects on soil invertebrates and terrestrial plants (Efroymson et al., 1997 a, b). The benchmark values are intended for screening level assessment, and variations in soil properties and plant species sensitivity will greatly affect toxicity. However, they are useful for indicating which contaminants may be of concern and worthy of further study of toxic response. Plant and invertebrate toxicity tests could be conducted in the laboratory to evaluate site-specific effects.

Bright-colored tailings pile in river channel below mill, barren of vegetation, OHV users in action

In addition to these benchmarks, the Coordinator may consider ranges for concentrations of metals and trace elements in soils that are considered phytotoxic (e.g., ranges in Kabata-Pendias and Pendias, 1992). As with the DOE thresholds, the ranges are useful for screening, but actual toxicity is dependent on site-specific conditions. Laboratory or field phytotoxicity tests could be conducted to evaluate site-specific effects. Trustees can also assess field vegetation to determine whether hazardous substances in soils may have caused adverse effects to biological resources. For example, if concentrations in soils are sufficient to have caused changes in vegetation cover, composition, growth rate, survival, or community structure, soils may be injured as a pathway to vegetation or habitat.

Biota – Aquatic Life Example

Aquatic Life Criteria (ALC) provide a screening level indication of toxicological injuries to fish and benthic invertebrates. An ALC assessment can be supplemented with an evaluation of toxicological thresholds derived from the literature. Depending on the circumstances, trustees might consider conducting site-specific toxicity tests to evaluate potential acute and chronic effects of contaminants. Laboratory toxicity testing is specified in the DOI regulations as a method of determining injury (43 CFR §11.62(f)(4)(i)(E)).

In developing toxicological thresholds, the Coordinator should consider indicator species and their relative sensitivities to contaminants, and those site-specific water quality conditions that may influence toxicity (e.g., hardness, calcium concentration, pH, dissolved organic carbon, alkalinity).

Sediment effect concentrations that are consensus predictors of toxicity to aquatic invertebrates (described above) can be used as a screening level indication of toxicological injuries to benthic invertebrates. Benthic macro-invertebrates themselves are used extensively to monitor the effects of contamination on aquatic systems. Benthic macro-invertebrates demonstrate individual level responses (e.g., mortality, reduced growth, reduced reproductive fitness) and community level responses (e.g., reduced density, reduced species richness, community shift to more tolerant species) to contaminants.

The Coordinator may use fish population data to evaluate whether spatial patterns of fish population density, diversity, and age structure are indicative of potential toxicological effects and fish injury. Fish populations in potentially affected stream reaches can be compared to fish populations in reference areas.

Biota – Wildlife Example

The Coordinator should refer to the injury definition of biological resources that is most commonly relevant to assessment of injury to wildlife: ". . . concentration of the substance sufficient to cause the biological resource or its offspring to have undergone at least one of the following adverse changes in viability: death, disease, behavioral abnormalities, cancer, genetic mutations, physiological malfunctions (including malfunctions in reproduction), or physical deformations."

The DOI NRDAR regulations list specific injury tests for demonstrating reductions in viability, but the Coordinator may need to develop specific tests for determination of injury to wildlife. Injury to wildlife can be determined by demonstrating that a particular biological response (such as death or a sub-lethal effect) meets "acceptance criteria" that link hazardous substances exposure to the observed effect.

To meet the acceptance criteria, the Coordinator must show that:

◆ The biological response is a commonly documented response resulting from exposure to oil or hazardous substances;

◆ Exposure to oil or hazardous substances is known to cause this biological response in controlled experiments and in free ranging organisms; and

◆ The biological response measurement is practical to perform and produces scientifically valid results.

Determination of injury to wildlife can be complicated, because wildlife may experience lethal effects, or sub-lethal injuries that are difficult to detect and measure. Coordinators might need to identify and engage individuals with specific expertise, such as wildlife biologists, toxicologists, and contaminants specialists within the BLM, other DOI bureaus, other Federal agencies, academia, and consultants, when designing studies to determine and quantify injuries to wildlife. In addition, if threatened or endangered species or species of special status are potentially injured, Coordinators should engage species-specific expertise to address any individuals or populations that occur on the BLM-managed lands. See *Risk Management Criteria for Metals at BLM Mining Sites* (Ford, 2004) for relevant information on toxicity to biota.

In the case of wildlife death, the Coordinator may find wildlife carcasses on which accepted techniques of necropsy, pathology, or other chemical analyses can demonstrate the cause of death from poisoning by the released substance. This may be compared to literature documentation that the substance is known to be toxic to both wild and laboratory animals.

In the case of sub-lethal effects, the Coordinator may observe changes in wildlife manner or behavior. For example, birds may no longer successfully fledge chicks in an area previously known to be a high-quality nesting area. In such a case, studies may be needed to evaluate whether the reduction in fledging success is related to chemical exposure, or to some other factor unrelated to the release. To design the studies, the Coordinator should keep in mind the acceptance criteria. Both field and laboratory investigations may be needed to determine whether the observed lack of fledging is real, whether it can be linked to hazardous substance exposure, and the spatial and temporal extents of the effect in the wild.

Determinations of injury to fish, wildlife, and birds should consider the extent of impact, i.e. whether individuals, local populations, or more widespread populations are affected by the release or spill. In determining and quantifying injury to wildlife, the Coordinator should be aware of the issue of "individual level" versus "population level" effects. The DOI regulations define resource injury at the level of individual organisms, but if losses of individuals reduce the level of service provided by lands managed by the BLM, then the Coordinator need not show a population level effect. PRPs have argued that an injury has not occurred if there is no population level effect.

Habitat

Habitat services are often the predominant concern for the BLM. Habitat services may be reduced from baseline levels when the resources are injured, and the amount of service loss is the reduction from baseline over the time period of injury. It is important to carefully identify the measure of service, such as acres of bird nesting or fishery user days. The time period may be from the beginning of injured condition until the resources return to baseline.

To assess injury to habitat, the Coordinator should compare key habitat components and services in the assessment area with those at reference sites. Injuries to habitat resulting from releases of hazardous substances are fairly common, because contaminants cycle among, and can adversely affect, many ecological components of a habitat. Examples of terrestrial components are soils, soil water, vegetation vigor, species composition, abundance, cover, structure, and seed production. Dependent habitat services that may be affected include, for example, forage quality and production, thermal cover or nesting opportunity. The Coordinator should look for direct injuries to individual a-biotic or biological components of the habitat, and also indirect effects that lead to losses of ecosystem stability, connectedness, or function.

Contaminant exposure can directly or indirectly injure one or more habitat components through toxicity effects. Loss of vegetation components can adversely affect wildlife that depends on the vegetation for forage, nesting, staging, hiding, or thermal cover. If contaminants cause changes in nutrient cycling that reduce plant productivity, plant cover, or community composition, then the services provided by the baseline community may be diminished. Loss of vegetation or a change in the type of vegetation can also lead to erosion of soils and stream banks, and subsequently affect biological communities that depend on unimpaired water or stable stream banks. Coordinators should consider such cascading or downstream effects on habitat, including the physical effects that result from the chemical impacts of a contaminant. The Coordinator also should consider that response actions may cause habitat service impacts.

If it is necessary to simplify an assessment, the Coordinator may be able to identify an indicator species in a habitat, if ecological associations between the indicator and other species can be scientifically established. For example, if the release causes toxicity to a plant species that is a major component of habitat for wildlife, then restoration is needed to reestablish conditions suitable for the growth of that plant, and thus the habitat services it provides for wildlife. In addition, if there is injury to wildlife from exposure to releases in habitat managed by the BLM, then the habitat may be injured as a pathway to wildlife.

APPENDIX E

Habitat Equivalency and Resource Equivalency Analysis and Metrics

1. HEA and REA

To determine how much habitat restoration is needed, the Coordinator may employ the HEA and REA methods to calculate the losses and the gains for impacted and restored habitats or resources. To determine the damages, the Coordinator would use the quantity of the cumulative loss of resources or services caused by the injury—the "debit"—and determine the equivalent amount of restoration or compensation needed--the "credit"--that is necessary to offset that resource injury or service loss. The cost of obtaining the "credit" (i.e., the compensation) becomes the damages relating to the loss of habitat services. Making this comparison depends directly on the Coordinator carefully identifying the metric of loss and the gain to be measured. In this way the Coordinator may directly compare losses and gains of specific natural resources (e.g., numbers of bald eagles) or acres of habitat services (e.g., wetland acres, nesting acres). Using this approach, equivalence can be established based on the sum of the losses caused by injuries and the sum of the gains from the restoration actions.

The Coordinator should scale the restoration or compensation so that the ecological service gains provided by the restoration or compensation are equivalent to the cumulative service losses at the injured site (NOAA, 2000). Scaling is the process of determining the appropriate size of a restoration project. When a "credit" from a restoration action matches or offsets the "debit" from the injury or loss, equivalence is achieved. This approach is simplest when the proposed restoration actions will replace or improve exactly the same type of natural resources and services that were lost. The technical approach for completing an HEA is presented in a series of published articles (e.g., NOAA, 2000; Jones and Pease, 1997; Unsworth and Bishop, 1994). If physical resources (e.g., numbers of birds or fish, or pounds of a contaminant) are selected as the metric for equivalency restoration, scaling is described as a REA. REA is a variation of HEA that was first introduced in 1999 on the North Cape oil spill (Sperduto et al., 1999). The concepts of the methods are similar, but the model parameters are different. REA requires life history information about the injured species like longevity and reproductive rates to identify the direct losses and indirect losses from foregone progeny.

HEA and REA models incorporate a time element, such as interim losses. They are used to compare the present value of all debits to the present value of all anticipated gains credits. The losses of services and the gains of services accrue over different time periods, and a unit of ecological services gained in the future is less valuable than a unit of ecological services that is available today. This is based on the economic reality that a unit of an asset is less valuable today than it was in the past, and more valuable today than it will be in the future. For the sake of calculation, all resource values are thus normalized to a specific year, often the case settlement year. To make past and future losses and gains comparable, calculations are made that discount the quantities of service from past or future years to present-day terms ("present value"). In accordance with OPA and CERCLA NRDAR regulations, HEA and REA calculations typically incorporate a discount rate of 3% for each year into the past and into the future, which has the effect of compounding past service loss and discounting future service loss compared to the present value. Common units in HEA are "service acre years" (SAYs), which become "discounted service acre years" (DSAYs) after factoring in the discounting for past and future years.

Use of HEA and REA has become commonplace in NRDAR because these methods lend themselves well to cooperative assessments and negotiated settlements of damages and restoration, particularly when total damages are relatively small or moderate.

2. Metrics for HEA

2.1 Examples of Metrics

The Coordinator should be careful to identify the appropriate metric, a single measurable attribute of a resource or service that has been injured or lost, when using HEA. The metric used to measure the injury or loss should be the same as, or sufficiently equivalent to, the one used to determine the restoration or compensation. For example, the metric should be an attribute about which the Coordinator can discern relative differences in the quality and quantity of the services provided by the injured, baseline, and compensatory (restored) habitats. Specific examples of metrics include:

◆   Measures of vegetative density, cover, diversity, or biomass, if any of these are keys to supporting wildlife and other services provided by the injured habitat. Depending on the specific services thought to be lost, the vegetative measure could be the percent cover of desirable, dominant, or essential vegetation species; the aboveground biomass of the dominant vegetation (for grasslands or wetlands); the density of seedlings (in areas where seedling recruitment is important); or an index of vegetation structural diversity (if the injury has caused a simplification of the structure of the habitat such that niche space has been lost).

◆   Indicators of rangeland health (Technical Reference # 1734-6). Soil stability, hydrologic function, and the site capacity to support characteristic, functional, and structural communities are indicators relevant to rangeland health.

◆   Habitat use-days, if an injury has reduced the availability of habitat such that fewer birds or other wildlife can occupy the habitat for essential needs, such as nesting. This measure might involve field surveys, such as bird point counts during key seasons, in affected and reference areas.

◆   Categories of service loss assigned based on the degree of exceedence of toxicity thresholds. This approach might involve compiling dose-response information from the literature or site-specific studies, and developing an estimate of service loss as a function of increasing contaminant concentration in soil, sediment, surface water, or biological tissues. Data or examples that link concentrations in media to adverse effects are helpful in supporting this approach.

2.2 Questions to identify HEA metrics.

In consultation with an economist and attorney, the Coordinator will typically be asked to respond to a number of questions relating to the specific resource injuries and to the intended restoration actions.

Evaluation of Damages

If the release area has a lot of unique characteristics that would require different restoration and compensation projects to provide commensurate services, then the area should be broken down into sub-sections. For *each* sub-section, the following questions need to be answered. Ranges of estimates are acceptable for sensitivity analysis. Please be sure to document the source(s) of the data for follow-up questions.

1.   How many acres (or some other unit of measure) were affected by the release?

2.   What are the percentage losses in ecosystem services from the release (e.g., 80% of the services have been destroyed; 20% functioning)?

3.   How many years and what level of productivity would you expect the area to return to if left alone (e.g., recover from 20% functioning to 50% maximum over 20 years)?

Primary Restoration/Remediation

1.   What primary restoration activities have been or will be undertaken, if any?

2.   If primary restoration activities are undertaken, what year would you expect or did the restoration project(s) start?

3.   How many years do you expect it will take the primary restoration project(s) to return ecological services to a maximum level of productivity (e.g., recover from 20% functioning to 80% maximum over 10 years)?

Compensatory Restoration

1.   What are the proposed compensatory restoration projects (e.g., habitat creation, stock fish, erosion control, buy land offsite)? Theoretical projects and restored services may be considered at the earliest stages of analysis.

2.   What year would you expect the compensatory restoration project(s) to start, if selected?

3.   How many years do you expect it will take the compensatory restoration projects to return what ecological services to a maximum level of productivity (e.g., restore to 80% maximum over 20 years)? (Please be sure to identify the percent services or the percent improvement in services if you have plans to enhance existing habitat.)

3. Example of Metrics for REA

Like HEA, REA is a replacement cost approach that seeks to measure how much it would cost to replace the natural resource services that the public lost as a result of the injury. In consultation with a case economist and attorney, the Coordinator will typically be asked to fill out injury, life history and demographic parameters for each injured species. Examples on the injury side are numbers of dead or injured individuals, normal individual life spans, time periods and annual rates of reproduction, and normal survival rates. Examples on the restoration side are numbers or rates of expected species replacement with restoration projects, such as reproduction and survivability rates, expected species number production from habitat acquisition or enhancement, or similar considerations.

www.ingramcontent.com/pod-product-compliance
Lightning Source LLC
Chambersburg PA
CBHW080308290526
45790CB00005B/1968

* 9 7 8 1 5 1 1 7 0 5 6 3 9 *